Budweiser

DODGE
Bud

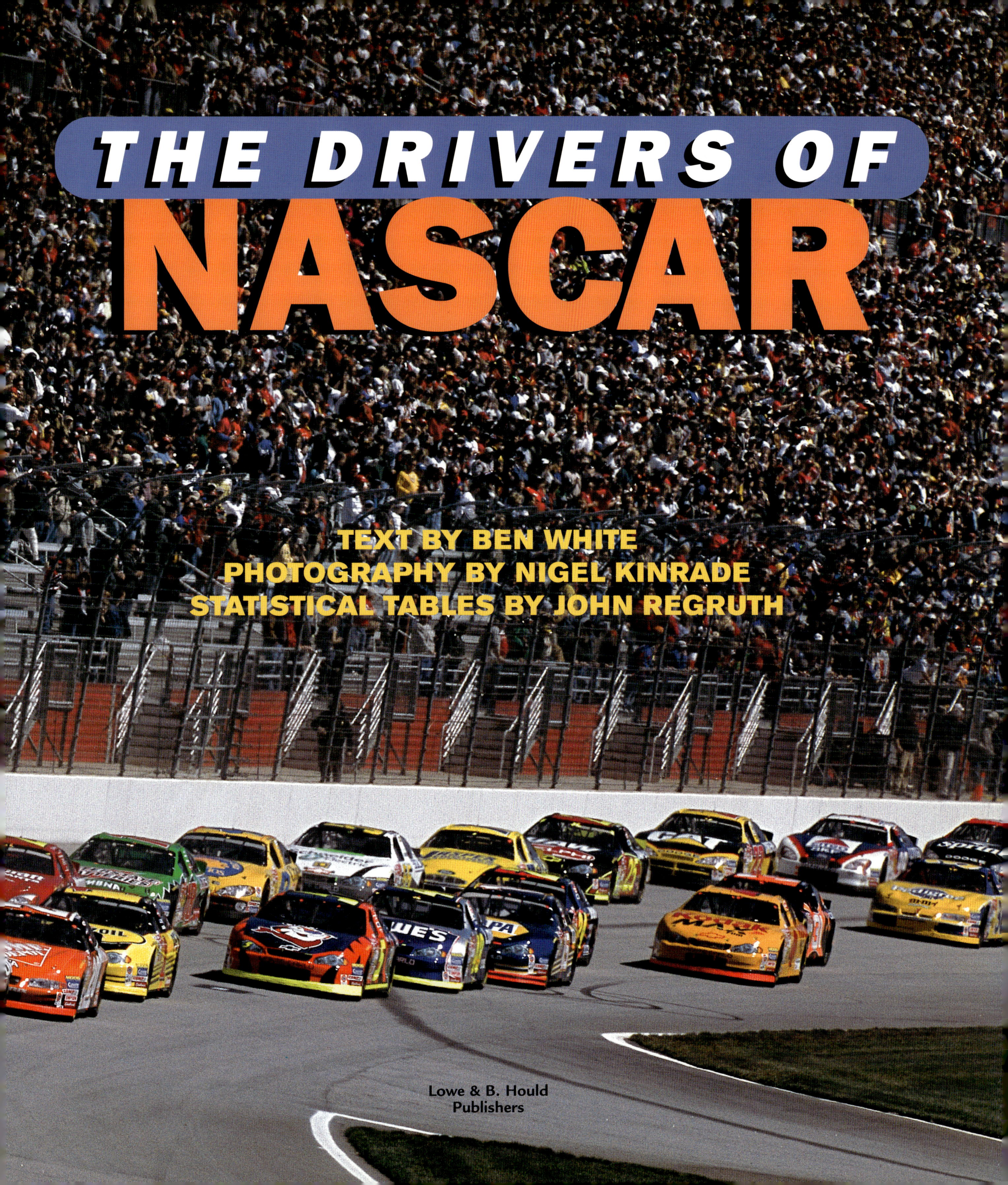

THE DRIVERS OF NASCAR

TEXT BY BEN WHITE
PHOTOGRAPHY BY NIGEL KINRADE
STATISTICAL TABLES BY JOHN REGRUTH

Lowe & B. Hould
Publishers

This edition published in 2002 by Lowe & B. Hould Publishers, an imprint of Borders, Inc., 515 East Liberty, Ann Arbor, MI 48104. Lowe & B. Hould Publishers is a trademark of Borders Properties, Inc.

First published in 2002 by MBI Publishing Company, Galtier Plaza, Suite 200, 380 Jackson Street, St. Paul, MN 55101-3885 USA

Library of Congress Cataloging-in-Publication Data Available

ISBN 0-681-78955-7

Printed in China

CONTENTS

ACKNOWLEDGMENTS

To my father, the late Ben Newton White Jr. Thank you, Dad, for introducing me to the exciting world of NASCAR Winston Cup racing.

First and foremost, I would like to thank the NASCAR Winston Cup drivers and teams featured in this book for the time they extended to me for this project, as well as past projects in my nearly 20 years of motorsports journalism. Your insight and continued friendship is most appreciated.

A tremendous thanks to Denny Darnell, Rob Goodman, and the entire staff of Sports Marketing Enterprises, R.J. Reynolds Tobacco Co., for helping to provide information both personal and professional concerning each subject featured here.

Hearty thanks to John Regruth for his great work in providing the statistical charts for each driver, and to Nigel Kinrade for his fantastic photographs, all of which are so central to this book. Josh Leventhal and Lee Klancher of MBI Publishing Company offered tremendous contributions toward making this book a success.

As always, I'd like to thank Mark Ashenfelter, Kenny Bruce, Rob Fisher, Jon Gunn, Rick Houston, Jeff Owens, Steve Waid, Ray Shaw, Whitney Shaw, Kirk Shaw, Art Weinstein, and Deb Williams of NASCAR Winston Cup Illustrated and NASCAR Winston Cup Scene for their continued support.

Finally, a very sincere thank you to my wife, Eva, and son, Aaron. You have no idea how much joy and happiness you bring to my life.

—Ben White

Above: Success in NASCAR Winston Cup racing requires a group effort. Here Bobby Labonte and his Pontiac get attention from the Joe Gibbs Racing team in pit row at Las Vegas Motor speedway in March 2002.

Below: The old guard and the new. Seven-time champion Dale Earnhardt Sr. and four-time champion Jeff Gordon enjoy a light moment late in the 1995 season. Gordon edged out Earnhardt for that year's Winston Cup title by a mere 34 points.

INTRODUCTION

Few of us get to experience the heart-pounding thrill of pushing a top-of-the-line stock car to its limits around a racetrack. Fewer still possess the elusive combination of skill, courage, and luck that it takes to be a NASCAR winner. As a result, millions of fans around the world look to these favored few as true heroes. So if fate hasn't seen fit to make us Winston Cup champions, then we ought at least be able to sit down and chew the fat with our idols of the ovals.

Here we offer an up-close-and-personal look at the leading stock car drivers of our time. Some have faced both glory in the Winner's Circle and near-death encounters on the oval over lengthy, perhaps legendary, careers. Others are so young they barely look old enough to drive. Some come to the sport from veritable racing dynasties with winning pedigrees; others emerged from obscure beginnings and fought mightily just for the chance to prove themselves on the track. The highest of triumphs and lowest of disappointments can be seen in the eyes of these men and women, their actions captured by the photographs within these pages.

Wherever they came from and whatever their background, all the men and women who slide through the window into the driver's seat of a Winston Cup car are motivated by the same force: the unrelenting desire to best a rival in a turn or down a straightaway, and reach the finish line in front of the rest.

Left: Jubilation! Dale Earnhardt Jr. celebrates a win at Texas Motor Speedway in 2000. The thrill of victory is what it's all about for today's great stock car drivers.

Top: Two legends of NASCAR compare notes before a race at Bristol Motor Speedway in 2000. Combined, the former champions Darrell Waltrip and Dale Jarrett have started more than 1,200 races.

Above: Under the helmet, all drivers are created equal. Shawna Robinson is the only female driver currently on the NASCAR Winston Cup Circuit, and the first woman to complete a race in more than two decades.

Cheerios
STP
NASCAR

JOHN ANDRETTI

43

Born:
March 12, 1963
Bethlehem, Pennsylvania

Height: 5-5

Weight: 140 lbs

Sponsor	**Cheerios**
Make	**Dodge**
Crew Chief	**Greg Steadman**
Owner	**Richard Petty**

NASCAR Winston Cup Career Statistics

Year	Races	Wins	Top 5s	Top 10s	Poles	Total Points	Final Standing	Winnings
1993	4	0	0	0	0	250	--	$24,915
1994	29	0	0	0	0	2,299	32nd	$391,920
1995	31	0	1	5	1	3,140	18th	$593,542
1996	30	0	2	3	0	2,621	31st	$688,511
1997	32	1	3	3	1	3,019	23rd	$1,143,725
1998	33	0	3	10	0	3,677	11th	$1,838,379
1999	34	1	3	10	0	3,394	17th	$2,001,832
2000	34	0	0	2	0	3,169	23rd	$2,035,902
2001	35	0	1	2	0	2,943	31st	$2,873,184
Totals	262	2	13	35	2	24,512		$11,591,910

Ask John Andretti what he would be doing if he weren't busy turning left every Sunday, and you might get an answer that surprises you. Without a doubt, he would much prefer to be working as an investment banker, settled comfortably behind a desk wearing a suit and tie. Having a name like "Andretti" on your business card—a name as synonymous with motorsports as "Arnold Palmer" is to professional golf—brings with it almost impossibly high expectations.

Every time the Pennsylvania native rolls his Petty Enterprises Dodge out of any garage area, his family's racing heritage rolls out with him. Given that the people for whom Andretti races come from their own racing dynasty built on another of the most recognized names in

John Andretti drives his Petty Enterprises Dodge low in the turns at California Speedway in April 2002.

Top: Peering through his helmet, Andretti awaits the start of a NASCAR event at Pocono International Raceway. Bottom Left: The Petty Enterprises crew does what they do best during a pit stop at Michigan in June 2000. Like all pit crews, they have their work down to a science. Bottom Right: Andretti takes a break between practice sessions at Bristol Motor Speedway in 1998. He proudly displays the STP colors.

Top: Wheeling the STP-sponsored No. 43 at Watkins Glen in 2000, Andretti puts his Pontiac through its left and right paces on the tough road course. Bottom: Andretti seems content in post-race interviews after a good run at Homestead International Speedway in November 2001.

motorsports, success for the Petty-Andretti partnership can be defined by nothing less than winning.

John Andretti brings more than his name to the track each weekend, however. He has driven just about everything on wheels. He began racing go-karts at age 11, and followed his famous uncle Mario (winner of both the Daytona 500 and Indianapolis 500) and his father, Aldo, in open-wheeled machines. When the time came for John to get some seat time and instruction, he attended Andre Pillett's driving school in Zolder, Belgium, with cousin Michael Andretti.

John won the 1982 Rookie of the Year award in the stock car division at Dorney Park and won his first stock car race that same year. In 1983, he won rookie honors in the USAC midget circuit. His CART open-wheel debut came in 1987. In 1988, Andretti ran the 24 Hours of Daytona with uncle Mario and cousin Michael. He also made his debut in the Indianapolis 500 in 1988, finishing 21st.

Wins came in the IMSA 24-Hour race at Daytona in 1989 and in the CART West Coast Grand Prix in Australia in 1991. He finished fifth in the Indy 500 in 1991 and made the semifinals in his first-ever NHRA Drag Racing Top Fuel event in 1993, beating defending champion Joe Amato. As previously noted, Andretti will drive anything on wheels.

Andretti has two NASCAR victories under his belt through the 2001 season, the first coming at Daytona in 1997, and then at Martinsville, Virginia, in 1999, to give the Pettys a long-awaited victory.

Andretti seemingly has found a home with Petty Enterprises. Even though he has only collected one win since joining the organization at the start of the 1998 Winston Cup season, many see the potential for Andretti and the Pettys to make further motorsports history with a season of more than one win in the win column. Now that the team has a season behind it learning the Dodge Intrepid, they can get down to the business of racing and producing good finishes.

"Petty Enterprises is a great organization with Kyle [Petty] at the helm," Andretti says. "We've won races before and we'll win them again. This team is going to return to winning races. Things are coming around."

JOHNNY BENSON

10

Born:
June 27, 1963
Grand Rapids, Michigan

Height: 6-0

Weight: 180 lbs

Sponsor	**Valvoline**
Make	**Pontiac**
Crew Chief	**James Ince**
Owner	**MBV Motorsports**

NASCAR Winston Cup Career Statistics

Year	Races	Wins	Top 5s	Top 10s	Poles	Total Points	Final Standing	Winnings
1996	30	0	1	6	1	3,004	21st	$947,080
1997	32	0	0	8	1	3,575	11th	$1,256,457
1998	32	0	3	10	0	3,160	20th	$1,360,335
1999	34	0	0	2	0	3,012	28th	$1,567,668
2000	33	0	3	7	0	3,716	13th	$1,841,324
2001	36	0	6	14	0	4,152	11th	$2,894,903
Totals	197	0	13	47	2	20,619		$9,867,767

Of all the NASCAR Winston Cup drivers campaigning in 2002, Johnny Benson, driver of the MBV Motorsports Pontiac, has come the closest to capturing a Winston Cup victory without actually getting a winner's trophy in his clutches. So many times in his six-year career, he has been in position to win, but circumstance has taken him out of the mix in the closing stages.

Benson got accustomed to winning when he won the 1993 American Speed Association championship and continued on in the Busch Series, where he won Rookie of the Year honors in 1994. He followed that by winning the 1995 Busch Series championship. It was clear he could battle fiercely against the sport's biggest names. There was no question he had a bright future ahead of him.

The Michigan native began his Winston Cup career with team owner Chuck Rider in 1996 before moving on to Jack Roush in 1998 and then Tim Beverly in 2000. Nelson Bowers purchased the team 18 races into the 2000 season. One of Benson's greatest runs came in the 2000 Daytona 500. He took the lead after making a two-tire stop and held it for 39 laps. He lost the lead with only four laps remaining, before finishing 12th.

"We've been on the verge of winning in Winston Cup competition for a long time, and one day soon we're going to find it," Benson says. "All the ingredients are there. We just have to put them in all the right places. Once you've found Victory Lane, other wins seem to come."

Above: Johnny Benson brings his Pontiac to a stop in the pits at Las Vegas Motor Speedway in March 2002. Left: Benson shows his serious side behind the wheel of his racecar prior to the start of the 2001 Daytona 500.

Ralphs
Racing Team

BRETT BODINE

11

Born:
January 11, 1959
Chemung, New York

Height: 5-7

Weight: 160 lbs

Sponsor	**Hooters Restaurants**
Make	**Ford**
Crew Chief	**Buddy Sisco**
Owner	**Brett Bodine**

You don't need television to see a series featuring a "survivor"—all you have to do is look Brett Bodine's way. Following in his brother Geoffrey's footsteps, Brett first joined NASCAR's elite circuit in 1986.

Brett Bodine had already established himself as a pretty good racecar driver when he came on the NASCAR scene, having won track modified championships at various venues across the Northeast. His racing career began in 1977 in hobby stocks at his home track of Chemung Speedway, in Chemung, New York. He worked his way up to the NASCAR Busch Series, where in 1986 he came close to winning the series championship, finishing second to Larry Pearson, son of NASCAR legend David Pearson.

In 1998, Bodine was named one of the top-50 modified drivers of all time. He drove for some of the most prominent team owners in the business, including Rick Hendrick, Hoss Ellington, Bud Moore, drag racer–turned–Winston Cup owner Kenny Bernstein, and the legendary driver-turned-owner, Junior Johnson. His lone victory to date came with Bernstein in 1990 in the First Union 400 at North Wilkesboro.

Bodine bought Johnson's team in 1996, and has served as the team's driver and owner ever since. At times, Bodine has struggled to keep the Winston Cup operation alive, but with the help of sponsor Bob Brooks and his Hooters Restaurant chain, Bodine has hopes for many more seasons of Winston Cup racing.

"Campaigning in Winston Cup racing is tough, but I wouldn't want to do anything else," Bodine says. "We're not as big as many of the teams we race against, but we've done some big things with fewer dollars."

NASCAR Winston Cup Career Statistics

Year	Races	Wins	Top 5s	Top 10s	Poles	Total Points	Final Standing	Winnings
1986	1	0	0	0	0	109	--	$10,100
1987	14	0	0	0	0	1,271	32th	$51,145
1988	29	0	2	5	0	2,833	20th	$433,658
1989	29	0	1	6	0	3,051	19th	$281,274
1990	29	1	5	9	1	3,440	12th	$442,681
1991	29	0	2	6	1	2,980	19th	$376,220
1992	29	0	2	13	1	3,491	15th	$495,224
1993	29	0	3	9	2	3,183	20th	$582,014
1994	31	0	1	6	0	3,159	19th	$791,444
1995	31	0	0	2	0	2,988	20th	$893,029
1996	30	0	0	1	0	2,814	24th	$767,716
1997	31	0	0	2	0	2,716	29th	$936,694
1998	33	0	0	0	0	2,907	25th	$1,281,673
1999	32	0	0	0	0	2,351	35th	$1,321,396
2000	29	0	0	0	0	2,145	35th	$1,020,659
2001	36	0	0	2	0	2,948	30th	$1,740,526
Totals	442	1	16	61	5	42,386		$11,425,453

Right: Brett Bodine is all set for a competitive run. This time, he's looking for a good finish at Atlanta Motor Speedway in November 2000. Below: Bodine takes the Hooters Ford around the bend at Lowe's Motor Speedway in May 2002.

ITGO

JEFF BURTON

99

Born:
June 29, 1967
South Boston, Virginia

Height: 5-7

Weight: 155 lbs

Sponsor	**Citgo**
Make	**Ford**
Crew Chief	**Frank Stoddard**
Owner	**Jack Roush**

NASCAR Winston Cup Career Statistics

Year	Races	Wins	Top 5s	Top 10s	Poles	Total Points	Final Standing	Winnings
1993	1	0	0	0	0	52	--	$9,550
1994	30	0	2	3	0	2,726	24th	$594,700
1995	29	0	1	2	0	2,556	32nd	$630,770
1996	30	0	6	12	1	3,538	13th	$884,303
1997	32	3	13	18	0	4,285	4th	$2,296,614
1998	33	2	18	23	0	4,415	5th	$2,626,987
1999	34	6	18	23	0	4,733	5th	$5,725,399
2000	34	4	15	22	1	4,836	3rd	$5,959,439
2001	36	2	8	16	0	4,394	10th	$4,230,737
Totals	259	17	81	119	2	31,535		$22,958,499

Jeff Burton, driver of the Roush Racing Ford, has had a taste of glory in his nine-year Winston Cup career. But like his fellow competitors, he won't be satisfied until he reaches the pinnacle of the sport with a Winston Cup championship.

In high school, Burton made a habit of excelling at every sport he entered, following the standard set by his favorite team, the Duke University Blue Devils. As he engaged in some pretty intense go-kart racing, his efforts improved enough to make him a two-time Virginia State champion by the age of seven. By his 17th birthday, in June 1984, Burton was racing the Pure Stock Class at South Boston Speedway, and four years later, he was winning races in double-digits in the track's premier Late Model Stock division.

Burton's first NASCAR win came at Martinsville, Virginia, in the Busch Series in 1990, and he went on to place 15th in points that season. By 1993, the urge to go on to Winston Cup racing was simply too great to ignore. His first start came on July 11 at New Hampshire International Speedway for team owner Filbert Martocci. Burton ran well in the opening laps, but fell out after crashing on lap 86 of the 300-lap event.

Right: Jeff Burton studies information given to him while behind the wheel of his Ford at Phoenix in October 2001. Below: Burton turns his Roush Racing Ford left on the concrete at Las Vegas in March 2002. A strong ninth-place finish there helped put Burton near the top early in the 2002 campaign.

Over time, Burton attracted attention from several prominent team owners, including Bill and Mickey Stavola, as well as Jack Roush, the organization from which all Burton's wins have come. His best season to date was 1999, when he logged 6 victories, 18 top fives, and 23 top 10s. Burton posted wins that year at Charlotte, both Darlington races, Las Vegas, Rockingham, North Carolina, and the spring race at New Hampshire, where it all began.

Going into the 2002 season, Burton has collected 17 victories since his first start in 1993, but even he might want to lock the 2001 season away in the history books. Sure, he won two events, at Charlotte and Phoenix, performances that helped him squeak out a 10th-place finish in the Winston Cup points race—but he also finished 11th or worse in 19 races that year. To win

Top: Burton makes a pit stop at Martinsville Speedway. Burton's Roush Racing crew is one of the fastest on the Winston Cup circuit. Middle: Burton races Davey Blaney (No. 93) for position at Dover Downs International Speedway in June 2001. Right: Burton takes aim with champagne in Victory Lane after winning at New Hampshire in July 1998.

a championship, a driver and team must hover around the top three positions all season long and never fall further back. Burton knew his chances for a championship in 2001 were pretty much out the window, considering his bad luck and Jeff Gordon's consistency week after week. Still, a top-10 finish in points certainly is an achievement about which a driver should be proud to brag.

"Ours wasn't the greatest year we've ever had, but we certainly had some high spots," Burton recalls. "Not all is going to go right during a season. You certainly want it to, but the odds are against that. Just have to keep trying, never give up, and do your best each week. That's how we were able to finish in the top 10 in points [in 2001]. We just didn't let the bad times get us down."

Right: Burton raises his arms in victory after besting the field at Phoenix International Speedway in November 2000. It was his fourth win of the season, helping Burton achieve his best year to date. Below: Behind the wheel of his Ford, Burton is set to get down to business in this 1998 photograph.

CAT
CAT

WARD BURTON 22

Born:
October 25, 1961
South Boston, Virginia

Height: 5-6

Weight: 150 lbs

Sponsor	**Caterpillar**
Make	**Dodge**
Crew Chief	**Tom Baldwin**
Owner	**Bill Davis**

Ward Burton has often been asked why his accent is so much different than that of younger brother Jeff. About all Ward can do is shrug his shoulders and say, "It's just the way I talk." Ward sounds like a Civil War Confederate general—his southern Virginia drawl is as thick and smooth as brown maple syrup. Brother Jeff has it all figured out. When a member of the motorsports media asked Jeff why there was a difference, Jeff replied, "Well, all I can figure is I was born in the northernmost point of the house and Ward was born in the southernmost part."

In the early 1970s, stock car racing came to the Burton family via radio broadcast every Sunday afternoon. Through the excitement of what he heard over the airwaves, Ward chose his all-time sports hero—Winston Cup champion Bobby Allison.

NASCAR Winston Cup Career Statistics

Year	Races	Wins	Top 5s	Top 10s	Poles	Total Points	Final Standing	Winnings
1994	26	0	1	2	1	1,971	35th	$304,700
1995	29	1	3	6	0	2,926	22nd	$634,655
1996	27	0	0	4	1	2,411	33rd	$873,619
1997	31	0	0	7	1	2,987	24th	$1,004,944
1998	33	0	1	5	2	3,352	16th	$1,516,183
1999	34	0	6	16	1	4,062	9th	$2,405,913
2000	34	1	4	17	0	4,152	10th	$2,699,604
2001	36	1	6	10	0	3,846	14th	$3,583,692
Totals	250	3	21	67	6	25,707		$13,023,310

Ward Burton is going full throttle at Las Vegas Motor Speedway in March 2002.

Since Allison used No. 12 on most of his cars, Burton claimed the number for his racecars, the go-karts he raced, and even on the back of his baseball and football jerseys.

Like his brother Jeff, Ward began racing go-karts at age eight and raced there until he was 16 years old. Mini-stocks and street stocks appealed to him until Late Model stocks caught his eye in 1986. By 1989, Burton earned three victories at South Boston, Virginia, as well as most-popular-driver honors. He finished second in the Rookie of the Year battle in the NASCAR Busch Series in 1990, although he eventually won four races in that division, a forum he continues to enter on occasion.

By 1994, Burton found an open door to the NASCAR Winston Cup circuit through team owner A. G. Dilliard, the father-in-law of driver Rick Mast. The following year, Burton joined Bill Davis, a successful Arkansas businessman who felt a deep passion for the Winston Cup circuit.

Burton capped 1995 with his first career victory, winning at Rockingham late in the season. From there, he scored wins at Darlington Raceway in the spring of 2000 and summer of 2001 in the prestigious Southern 500.

In 2002, Burton stepped his career up to a new plateau by claiming victory at the Daytona 500. When the checkered flag waved after a fierce 200 circuits around Daytona International Speedway, Burton had escaped an afternoon of wrecks to score not only his own biggest victory but also the biggest victory in the 16-year history of Bill Davis Racing. The victory meant a lot to Burton for its historic value.

"When I was growing up, I followed all the greats, such as Bobby Allison, Cale Yarborough, Richard Petty, David Pearson, all of them," Burton says. "I remember when each one of them won the Daytona 500, and to be put in that same category is just simply unreal."

Burton waves to the crowd at pre-race introductions before the start of the Coca-Cola 600 at Charlotte in May 1999.

Left: At Martinsville Speedway in April 2001, Ward Burton battles younger brother Jeff (No. 99) in front of a group of cars wanting their positions. Middle: Burton's eyes tell the story as he awaits the start of a Winston Cup event at Michigan in 1999. Bottom Left: Burton is all smiles during a conversation at Pocono International Speedway in July 1999. Bottom Right: Burton enjoys the flat concrete surface of Martinsville Speedway, a place where he has seen much success.

NASCAR
Winston Cup
Series
Kenmore
SIMPSON
Downy
Ford
RACING
100 YEARS
Tide
Tide
SUPER
8
MOTEL

RICKY CRAVEN

32

Born:
May 24, 1966
Newburgh, Maine

Height: 5-9

Weight: 165 lbs

Sponsor	**Tide**
Make	**Ford**
Crew Chief	**Mike Beam**
Owner	**Cal Wells**

NASCAR Winston Cup Career Statistics

Year	Races	Wins	Top 5s	Top 10s	Poles	Total Points	Final Standing	Winnings
1991	1	0	0	0	0	61	--	$3,750
1995	31	0	0	4	0	2,883	24th	$597,054
1996	31	0	3	5	2	3,078	20th	$941,959
1997	30	0	4	7	0	3,108	19th	$1,259,550
1998	11	0	0	1	1	907	46th	$527,875
1999	24	0	0	0	0	1,513	41st	$853,835
2000	16	0	0	0	0	1,175	44th	$636,562
2001	36	1	4	7	1	3,379	21st	$1,996,981
Totals	180	1	11	24	4	16,104		$6,817,566

See a Winston Cup competitor sporting an orange-and-white uniform and a huge smile on his face, it's a good bet that you're looking at Ricky Craven, driver of the PPI Motorsports Ford. Since winning his first Winston Cup race in October 2001, Craven has not been able to hide those pearly whites.

The native of Bangor, Maine, likes what he sees these days in a career that has been revitalized with a team owned by Cal Wells. His cars are good. His team is good. Everyone seems to be mentioning Craven's name as the driver to beat in events on the Winston Cup schedule, especially at New Hampshire International Raceway, a track he considers his home turf. He has finally found a bit of stability in a personal racing venture that has seen its fair share of turbulence over its 11 years. One needs to look back at Craven's past to truly appreciate his present role with the Wells team.

Craven drove one event for Dick Moroso in 1991, 62 events for owner Larry Hedrick in 1995 and 1996, and then moved over to the prominent Charlotte-based Hendrick Motorsports and team owner Rick Hendrick, for whom he competed in 38 races. A couple of hard crashes with Hedrick's operation in 1996 and Hendrick in 1997 caused some head injuries that heavily influenced Craven's ability behind the controls. After Craven completed only four events in 1998, doctors determined that he was suffering from post-concussion syndrome, a side effect from the terrible spill he took in a multi-car crash at Talladega and a crash during a practice session at Texas. From there, many months of recuperation passed as he tried desperately to keep his driving hopes alive.

Craven managed to run three events late in the 1998 season with Nelson Bowers, and 24 total events for Scott Barbour and Hal Hicks in 1999. Unfortunately, the strong finishes simply didn't come. So when Cal Wells cut driver Scott Sharp from his program and tapped Craven to fill

Ricky Craven puts his PPI Motorsports Ford to the test at North Carolina Speedway at Rockingham in February 2001.

Above: Craven glides along on the low side of Martinsville's near-flat turns in April 2001. Right: Craven displays his first official winner's trophy after his victory at Martinsville in 2001. Below: Looking a bit tired after a long day at Phoenix International Raceway late in the 2001 season, Craven finished well back after being taken out in an accident not of his making.

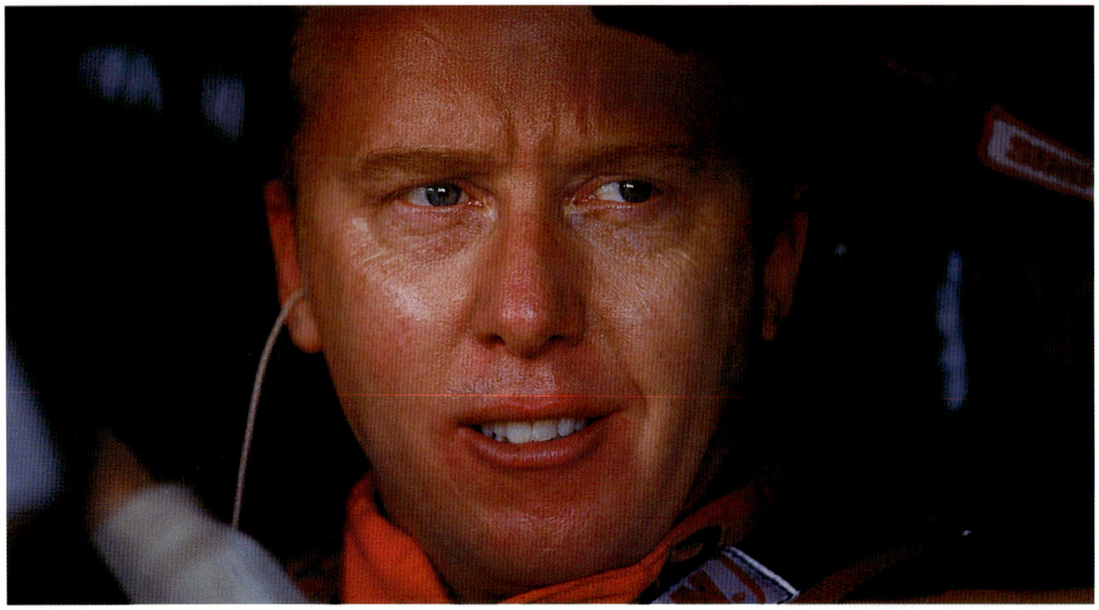

In October 2001 at Martinsville Speedway, Craven finally collected his first career Winston Cup victory after a long, hard-fought battle with Dale Jarrett.

the void, it was the break Craven had been searching for his entire career.

At the start of the 2002 season, Craven suffered mechanical difficulties at Daytona and had to start the 500 dead last in the 43-car field. Later, at Rockingham, Craven had his car running near perfectly, bringing him the fifth pole position of his career. (Two others came at New Hampshire, one at Martinsville, and one at Michigan Speedway in 2001.) Craven is definitely back on top of his game.

"I'd say this is the best situation I've had since I joined the Winston Cup circuit some years ago," Craven remarks. "I really feel [2002] is my best opportunity to race yet, and now that we've got one win behind us, I know the wins will come. I've waited a long time to get a ride this good, and I'm going to do all I can to find Victory Lane."

GM
Goodwrench Service Plus
Goodwrench Service Plus
BURGER KING
Snap-on
GOODYEAR
76
RCR
Goodwrench Service Plus
NASCAR Winston Cup Series
7-TIME CHAMPION
Coca-Cola
Team REALTREE
ACDelco
SIMPSON
Bass Pro Shops
PERDUE
GM
Goodwrench Service Plus

DALE EARNHARDT

3

Born:
April 29, 1951
Kannapolis, North Carolina

Height: 6-1

Weight: 180 lbs

Sponsor	**GM Goodwrench**
Make	**Chevrolet**
Crew Chief	**Kevin Hamline**
Owner	**Richard Childress**

For legions of stock car racing fans around the world, February 18, 2001, will forever be known as "Black Sunday." On that fateful day, the life and career of legendary driver Dale Earnhardt came to a sudden and tragic end during the final lap of the Daytona 500. A hero to fans and colleagues alike, Earnhardt's passing touched the world of NASCAR as deeply as anything.

The image of "The Intimidator" and "The Man in Black" shook some of the best drivers in the business. The black-and-silver No. 3 Chevrolet was one of the most feared images to show up in the rearview mirror of any NASCAR driver for more than two decades. It was not a question of whether Earnhardt could pass, but rather when he would pass. In the end, the black No. 3 came to symbolize the best stock car driver who ever lived.

The path to stock car racing greatness was set from Earnhardt's early childhood in Kannapolis, North Carolina. After all, it was in his blood. His father Ralph Earnhardt was a longtime racer and 1956 Sportsman champion, and Dale decided early on to pursue that same competitive streak. Although father and son were nearly divided by the younger Earnhardt's decision to quit school in ninth grade to devote his every breath to racing, father and son eventually patched their differences. Dale relied heavily on his father's expertise to help build his fledgling career.

During his second year of driving, Dale won 26 races and appeared to be on his way. Even more wins came in his third year. Suddenly, in September 1973, Ralph Earnhardt died of a massive heart attack at age 45, leaving behind a 19-year-old son unsure of where to turn; Earnhardt had expected his father and mentor to be at his side for many years to come.

NASCAR Winston Cup Career Statistics

Year	Races	Wins	Top 5s	Top 10s	Poles	Total Points	Final Standing	Winnings
1975	1	0	0	0	0	97	--	$1,925
1976	2	0	0	0	0	176	--	$3,085
1977	1	0	0	0	0	49	--	$1,375
1978	5	0	1	2	0	660	41st	$20,145
1979	27	1	11	17	4	3,749	7th	$264,086
1980	31	5	19	24	0	4,661	1st	$588,926
1981	31	0	9	17	0	3,975	7th	$347,113
1982	30	1	7	12	1	3,402	12th	$375,325
1983	30	2	9	14	0	3,732	8th	$446,272
1984	30	2	12	22	0	4,265	4th	$616,788
1985	28	4	10	16	1	3,561	8th	$546,596
1986	29	5	16	23	1	4,468	1st	$1,783,880
1987	29	11	21	24	1	4,696	1st	$2,099,243
1988	29	3	13	19	0	4,256	3rd	$1,214,089
1989	29	5	14	19	0	4,164	2nd	$1,435,730
1990	29	9	18	23	4	4,430	1st	$3,083,056
1991	29	4	14	21	0	4,287	1st	$2,396,685
1992	29	1	6	15	1	3,574	12th	$915,463
1993	30	6	17	21	2	4,526	1st	$3,353,789
1994	31	4	20	25	2	4,694	1st	$3,300,733
1995	31	5	19	23	3	4,580	2nd	$3,154,241
1996	31	2	13	17	2	4,327	4th	$2,285,926
1997	32	0	7	16	0	4,216	5th	$2,151,909
1998	33	1	5	13	0	3,928	8th	$2,990,749
1999	34	3	7	21	0	4,492	7th	$3,048,236
2000	34	2	13	24	0	4,865	2nd	$4,918,886
2001	1	0	0	0	0	132	--	$296,833
Totals	676	76	281	428	22	93,962		$41,641,084

The black-and-silver Chevrolet made famous by Dale Earnhardt will forever be etched in the minds of all race fans. Here, Earnhardt is at speed at Bristol Motor Speedway in March 2000.

One of Earnhardt's greatest wins came in October 2000 at Talladega Superspeedway. That day, he went from 18th to first in only three laps. It was Earnhardt's 76th and final victory.

The young Earnhardt struggled to break into Winston Cup racing on his own. Through the efforts of several team owners and crews, he was given an occasional opportunity to showcase his talents. By 1979, he took home Rookie of the Year honors with team owner Rod Osterland, and then scored the first of his seven Winston Cup championships a year later.

In midseason 1981, Osterland unexpectedly sold his team to coal magnate J. D. Stacy without consulting with his driver or crew, a move that devastated Earnhardt. After some careful thought, Earnhardt quit the team in May to take a ride vacated by longtime campaigner Richard Childress. The duo showed promise, but Childress felt that Earnhardt's talents as driver outweighed the equipment he was able to offer.

Two seasons with Bud Moore in Fords provided a few wins, but by 1984, Earnhardt was back with Childress. The combination went on to be one of the most successful unions in NASCAR history. They amassed a mind-boggling 6 Winston Cup championships, 69 wins, 17 pole positions, and nearly $50 million in race winnings over 17 seasons.

Even more than a year after his death, many fans and competitors continue to struggle with the idea that Dale Earnhardt is no longer a part of stock car racing. But good times and great racing remain his legacy, ultimately outweighing the impact of his tragic end.

"That's the way I remember Dale Earnhardt, the good times we had," Childress recalled in *NASCAR Winston Cup Scene*. "All the good things we've done. Those are the things I remember, that's the way I want to remember Dale and that's the way I'm going to remember him. I don't want to go back (to special places we visited) and sit and think about the tragedy that's happened."

Top Left: Often coming across as cocky and intense, Earnhardt was in truth warm and personable to those who knew him, but with a competitive spirit that put him in a league of his own on the track. Right: Earnhardt was famous for holding court with anyone who would listen. He was considered one of the wisest men in the garage area and was often consulted by NASCAR for advice. Left: Earnhardt always stood tall, whether in a photograph or in real life. Bottom Left: Earnhardt enjoyed finally winning the Daytona 500 in 1998 after coming so close to that elusive victory for a period of 20 years. Bottom Right: Earnhardt beats out Bobby Labonte for a win at Atlanta in March 2000. When the two got to the finish line, Earnhardt was the victor by a bumper.

Bud
KING OF BEERS

DALE EARNHARDT JR.

8

Born:
October 10, 1974
Kannapolis, North Carolina

Height: 6-0

Weight: 165 lbs

Sponsor	**Budweiser**
Make	**Chevrolet**
Crew Chief	**Tony Eury Sr.**
Owner	**DEI**

NASCAR Winston Cup Career Statistics

Year	Races	Wins	Top 5s	Top 10s	Poles	Total Points	Final Standing	Winnings
1999	5	0	0	1	0	500	48th	$162,095
2000	34	2	3	5	2	3,516	16th	$2,801,880
2001	36	3	9	15	2	4,460	8th	$5,827,542
Totals	75	5	12	21	4	8,476		$8,791,517

When the media scouted the new talent coming into the Winston Cup Series in 1999, it came as little surprise to find the name "Dale Earnhardt Jr." on the list of rookies. What came as a complete surprise to everybody was that a mere two years later, Dale Jr. would be the only Earnhardt on the circuit.

In the wake of the tragic death of his father at Daytona in February 2001, Earnhardt Jr. was looking to carry on the Earnhardt legacy in NASCAR's premier arena without his famous father at his side offering advice and encouragement. Throughout the rest of that 2001 season, Dale Jr. was a man everyone looked to for strength.

Early photos of Earnhardt Jr. feature him in one of the black-and-gray pit crew uniforms of the RCR Enterprises team his father drove for. Long before he was old enough to possess a North Carolina driver's license, Earnhardt Jr. had his sights set on becoming a racecar driver just like his dad. So serious was he about his venture that he and brother Kerry pulled an old 1978

Right: Dale Earnhardt Jr. enjoys an unexpected beer shower in Victory Lane at Richmond, Virginia, in May 2000. It was his second win that season. Below: The red-and-white No. 8 Chevy has come to symbolize Dale Earnhardt Jr. as much as the black-and-silver No. 3 was made famous by his father, the late Dale Earnhardt Sr.

Chevrolet Monte Carlo from the woods and welded roll bars within its stripped interior. Worried that the car wouldn't be safe, their father decided to help his young sons and began offering racing advice. Still, he wanted them to work on their own cars to learn the mechanical side of what makes them go fast.

After a few years campaigning on the short tracks around his Mooresville, North Carolina, home, Earnhardt Jr. was ready to try his hand on the superspeedways. He earned a Busch Series ride with Dale Earnhardt Inc. in 1996. He started that first event at Myrtle Beach in 7th position and finished 14th. The powerhouse started by his late father and stepmother Teresa in 1995 came to be a racing home for Earnhardt Jr. He rewarded them with back-to-back Busch Series championships, in his first year and again in 1999.

The inevitable rise to the Winston Cup ranks came in 1999, when he drove five events. The following year he competed for Rookie of the Year honors, but fell shy to Matt Kenseth by a mere 42 points. When

Left: Waving to his fans during driver introductions at Charlotte, Earnhardt Jr. has quickly gained a large following of admirers. Bottom Left: Shown here in September 1999, Earnhardt Jr. is set and ready for action. He was one of the last drivers to move from an open-face to full-face helmet. Bottom Right: Earnhardt Jr. lifts his first career winner's trophy after taking the big prize at Texas Motor Speedway in 2000.

Left: With his car low and at full speed, Earnhardt Jr. does what he does best: racing in Winston Cup competition. Below: In a very short period of time, Dale Jr. established himself as a winning driver. He claimed his second straight NASCAR Busch Series title at the close of the 1999 season.

Dale Jr. won his first career Busch Series race in his 16th start, his father was there to celebrate in Victory Lane. And when he won his first Winston Cup race in April of 2000, his father was there, too, as a competitor. The victory celebration was one to remember. Earnhardt Jr. paid homage to his father one more time by winning "The Winston" special non-points event for drivers who had won races during the previous season.

In 2001, Earnhardt Jr. achieved three emotional victories. First was the win at Daytona in July, the place of his father's death just a few months earlier. The second win came at Dover in the first NASCAR event after the September 11 terrorist attacks on New York City and Washington. The third came at Talladega, Alabama, the sight of his father's final career victory.

Many people consider Dale Earnhardt Jr. to be a viable candidate for winning a Winston Cup championship. His first two full seasons saw him finish 16th and 8th in the point standings. It seems only a matter of time before Dale Jr. joins his father on the list of NASCAR champions.

"We're moving forward with a great race team," Earnhardt Jr. says. "We can win championships because that's what Dale Earnhardt was about and what Dale Earnhardt Inc. is about."

NASCAR
Winston Cup
Champion
DODGE
Your Friendly

BILL ELLIOTT

9

Born:
October 8, 1955
Dawsonville, Georgia

Height: 6-1

Weight: 185 lbs

Sponsor	**Dodge Dealers**
Make	**Dodge**
Crew Chief	**Mike Ford**
Owner	**Ray Evernham**

Former Winston Cup champion Bill Elliott is enjoying one last resurgence in his 26-year NASCAR career before finally retiring to the north Georgia mountains where he was raised. A victory late in the 2001 season at Homestead, Florida—the 41st win of his career—ended a six-year winless streak. When the checkered flag fell over his Ray Evernham–owned Dodge, it silenced the critics who claimed that Elliott was simply too old to find Victory Lane again.

Stock car racing has been all the redhead from Georgia has ever known. He and his brothers Ernie and Dan got started early, scrounging around their father's junkyard and fixing up old cars that were perfect for racing—around the dirt roads between junk piles, that is. The boys of George and Mildred Elliott had found their calling.

With George acting as an early sponsor and financier, the fledgling race team spent summer weekends competing on small dirt tracks. The brothers eventually persuaded their father to buy a Winston Cup machine, a beat-up old Ford Torino purchased from Bobby Allison. The boys first raced the car at Rockingham, North Carolina, on February 29, 1976, with Bill finishing 33rd in his Winston Cup debut. Still, the boys felt rich with the $640 in prize money they collected.

They struggled mightily for the next few years and threatened more than once to close the doors on the team for good. Thankfully, businessman Harry Melling entered the picture, provided the Elliotts with top-notch equipment, and the wins began to come.

The first victory finally came in the last race of the 1983 season at Riverside, California, young Elliott's 117th career start. He posted three more wins in 1984 to set the stage for an incredible 1985 season. Bill won 11 races in 28 starts, starting his as-

NASCAR Winston Cup Career Statistics

Year	Races	Wins	Top 5s	Top 10s	Poles	Total Points	Final Standing	Winnings
1976	7	0	0	0	0	556	49th	$11,635
1977	10	0	0	2	0	1,002	36th	$20,575
1978	10	0	0	5	0	1,176	34th	$42,065
1979	14	0	1	5	0	1,709	28th	$57,450
1980	11	0	0	4	0	1,232	35th	$42,545
1981	13	0	1	7	1	1,442	31st	$70,320
1982	21	0	8	9	1	2,718	25th	$226,780
1983	30	1	12	22	0	4,279	3rd	$479,965
1984	30	3	13	24	4	4,377	3rd	$660,226
1985	28	11	16	18	11	4,191	2nd	$2,433,187
1986	29	2	8	16	4	3,844	4th	$1,069,142
1987	29	6	16	20	8	4,202	2nd	$1,619,210
1988	29	6	15	22	6	4,488	1st	$1,574,639
1989	29	3	8	14	2	3,774	6th	$854,570
1990	29	1	12	16	2	3,999	4th	$1,090,730
1991	29	1	6	12	2	3,535	11th	$705,605
1992	29	5	14	17	2	4,068	2nd	$1,692,381
1993	30	0	6	15	2	3,774	8th	$955,859
1994	31	1	6	12	1	3,617	10th	$936,779
1995	31	0	4	11	2	3,746	8th	$996,816
1996	24	0	0	6	0	2,627	30th	$716,506
1997	32	0	5	14	1	3,836	8th	$1,607,827
1998	32	0	0	5	0	3,305	18th	$1,618,421
1999	34	0	1	2	0	3,246	21st	$1,624,101
2000	32	0	3	7	0	3,267	21st	$2,580,823
2001	36	1	5	9	2	3,824	15th	$3,618,017
Totals	659	41	160	294	51	81,834		$27,306,174

Bill Elliott's red Ray Evernham Dodges proudly carry the number 9. Elliott first made that number famous in Fords owned by the late Harry Melling in the mid-1980s.

sault by dominating the Daytona 500. He won at Atlanta and Darlington, and overwhelmed the competition at Talladega in May, winning the pole position with a speed of 202.398 miles per hour. He broke an oil line during the race, but made up 5 miles under green conditions by turning lap after lap at more than 205 miles per hour, regaining the lost deficit to win the race.

The come-from-behind victory at Talladega was his second win of the four major NASCAR events. To win three meant he would be awarded a $1 million bonus from series sponsor R.J. Reynolds. Elliott suffered brake problems at the next $1 million eligible event at Charlotte, but came back at Darlington to win the Southern 500 and the bonus. No other driver has claimed the bonus since Elliott accomplished the feat in its inaugural year.

Top: During the years he held the roles of both driver and team owner, the Georgia native has worn many hats. Left: Elliott likes the response he hears when introduced to the fans at Charlotte in May 2001. His career has enjoyed a nice resurgence in his later years. Right: With his son Chase, Elliott smiles for the cameras after the elder Elliott won one of two 125-mile qualifying events prior to the 2000 Daytona 500.

In August 1987, Elliott turned the fastest time in a stock car, reaching 212.809 miles per hour at Talladega. He was crowned Winston Cup champion in 1988. From 1995 to 2000, Elliott again fielded his own cars with co-owner Charles Hardy, but the two never could break into the Winner's Circle. When Elliott joined Evernham at the start of the 2001 season, veteran motorsports writers were predicting them to win multiple races and billed them as a dream team of sorts. The multi-wins didn't come, but Elliott did prove that he could still win.

"It takes time to build a race team good enough to win, so to do that in the first year was pretty remarkable," Elliott says. "It just felt so good to get back to Victory Lane and show people I could still win races."

Top Left: Elliott signs an autograph for one of his many fans. Elliott has been named the National Motorsports Press Association Driver of the Year on 13 occasions. Top Right: Elliott poses for the cameras at Rockingham, North Carolina, in the early months of the 1997 Winston Cup season. That year, Elliott drove his own Fords that were housed in Dawsonville, Georgia. Bottom Left: Elliott's Dodge is one of the most recognizable racecars on the track. Here, he is pushing the throttle at Atlanta in March 2002.

NASCAR
Winston Cup
QUAKER STATE
GMAC
Tyvek
Fritos
DELPHI
LOWE'S

JEFF GORDON

24

Born:
August 4, 1971
Vallejo, California

Height: 5-7

Weight: 150 lbs

Sponsor	**DuPont**
Make	**Chevrolet**
Crew Chief	**Robbie Loomis**
Owner	**Rick Hendrick**

Not since Richard "The King" Petty first showed up on the NASCAR grids in 1958 has such a young driver shown, and gone on to fulfill, such overwhelming promise as Jeff Gordon. By the time he was 30 years old, Gordon had four Winston Cup titles under his belt—only the third driver ever to win that many—and he is widely considered the man most likely to break Petty's record of seven championships. With his good looks and astounding success, Gordon has established himself as a household name to both veteran fans and schoolchildren.

Gordon's talent showed itself early. The Vallejo, California, native began his racing career at age five in quarter midgets and go-karts. Over the next 15 years, awards and records fell to Gordon like dominos in every mode of open-wheel short-track racing.

When he was still a teenager, Gordon garnered offers from prestigious teams in several forms of auto racing, including one from former Formula One world champion Jackie Stewart. In the end, Gordon chose stock cars.

He attended the Buck Baker Driving School in early 1990 and simply loved the experience. With pillows stuffed inside a seat clearly too big for him, Gordon quickly got a handle on the heavier, bulkier stock cars and was turning some impressive times by the end of the day.

In his first year in the Busch Series division, Gordon won 1991 Rookie of the Year honors driving for owner Bill Davis. In 1992, he won 11 Busch Series pole positions and scored 3 victories. When he was ready to make his Winston Cup debut at the final

NASCAR Winston Cup Career Statistics

Year	Races	Wins	Top 5s	Top 10s	Poles	Total Points	Final Standing	Winnings
1992	1	0	0	0	0	70	--	$6,285
1993	30	0	7	11	1	3,447	14th	$765,168
1994	31	2	7	14	1	3,776	8th	$1,779,523
1995	31	7	17	23	8	4,614	1st	$4,347,343
1996	31	10	21	24	5	4,620	2nd	$3,428,485
1997	32	10	22	23	1	4,710	1st	$6,375,658
1998	33	13	26	28	7	5,328	1st	$9,306,584
1999	34	7	18	21	7	4,620	6th	$5,858,633
2000	34	3	11	22	3	4,361	9th	$3,001,144
2001	36	6	18	24	6	5,112	1st	$10,879,757
Totals	293	58	147	190	39	40,658		$45,748,580

Jeff Gordon takes to the treacherous 1.366-mile Darlington Raceway. On this occasion in March 2002, he finished a disappointing ninth, but Gordon has been victorious on five occasions at the track since 1992.

Top: A popular target for the media, Gordon takes a moment to speak to photographers at Daytona in 1998. Above: Gordon makes a scheduled pit stop for tires and fuel while racing his Hendrick Motorsports Chevrolet at Martinsville in 2001.

event of the 1992 season at Atlanta, he had to get written permission from his parents, since he was not yet 21 years old. He finished unremarkably, in 31st place, but his career soon took off after being signed to a Winston Cup contract by owner Rick Hendrick for the 1993 season.

Gordon established himself in the Winston Cup ranks immediately. He was named Rookie of the Year in 1993 and earned the distinction of becoming the youngest driver to win a 125-mile qualifying race at Daytona International Speedway.

Gordon started his 1994 season by winning the Busch Clash. He grabbed his first Winston Cup win at the Coca-Cola 600 at Charlotte Motor Speedway in May, and followed that with a victory in the Brickyard 400 at Indianapolis Motor Speedway in August, making him the first stock car driver to grace Indy's coveted victory circle.

In 1995, only his third full season, Gordon accomplished the unthinkable by winning the Winston Cup championship over the likes of Dale Earnhardt, Terry Labonte, and Rusty Wallace. He was the youngest Winston Cup champion in the modern era (since 1972) and the second youngest ever (1950 NASCAR champion Bill Rexford was only a few months younger). Gordon went on to collect further Winston Cup championships in 1997, 1998, and 2001 to become the winningest active driver.

"This team is stronger than it's ever been," Gordon says of his Robbie Loomis–led organization. "Obviously, the 2001 season was a great and awesome season since we were able to capture our fourth Winston Cup championship. But as good as this team is and as hard as they work, I'm certain we'll have more championships in the future. We always go into a season expecting to win the championship and a lot of preparation is the key to that."

Left: In August 1998, Gordon celebrated his second career victory in the prestigious Brickyard 400 at Indianapolis Motor Speedway. Top Right: Hidden behind his familiar multicolored helmet, Gordon gathers his thoughts before race time. Bottom Right: Looking more like someone who should be flipping burgers at the local drive-through than a man at the top of his sport, a young Gordon gleefully accepts his first championship trophy in November 1995. It was the first of four—and counting.

GARGOYLES
NASCAR
Winston Cup
Series

BOBBY HAMILTON

55

Born:
May 29, 1957
Nashville, Tennessee

Height: 6-0

Weight: 180 lbs

Sponsor	**Square D**
Make	**Chevrolet**
Crew Chief	**Charley Pressley**
Owner	**Andy Petree**

Bobby Hamilton's career in NASCAR Winston Cup began in a rather unique way. While most drivers get their break via newspaper headlines proclaiming their accomplishments on the track, Hamilton started along his path as a stunt double, of sorts, in the 1990 film *Days of Thunder*. Hamilton actually performed too well for the part. His role was to enter a race but not be scored as an actual participant. He qualified a Hendrick Motorsports–prepared Chevrolet in fifth and was running strong in the top 10 when NASCAR officials forced him to go to the garage area. And that wasn't Hamilton's first taste of show business. His father and grandfather built and maintained racecars for country music singer Marty Robbins.

Young Bobby Hamilton had often heard of drivers Darrell Waltrip and Sterling Marlin, two of NASCAR's greatest who once raced at Hamilton's hometown track, Nashville Speedway. When Hamilton won

NASCAR Winston Cup Career Statistics

Year	Races	Wins	Top 5s	Top 10s	Poles	Total Points	Final Standing	Winnings
1989	1	0	0	0	0	72	--	$3,075
1990	3	0	0	0	0	168	--	$13,065
1991	28	0	0	4	0	2,915	22nd	$59,105
1992	29	0	0	2	0	2,787	25th	$367,065
1993	15	0	0	1	0	1,348	37th	$142,740
1994	30	0	0	1	0	2,749	23rd	$514,520
1995	31	0	4	10	0	3,576	14th	$804,505
1996	31	1	3	11	2	3,639	9th	$1,151,235
1997	32	1	6	8	2	3,450	16th	$1,478,843
1998	33	1	3	8	1	3,786	10th	$2,089,566
1999	34	0	1	10	0	3,564	13th	$2,019,255
2000	34	0	0	2	0	2,715	30th	$1,619,775
2001	36	1	3	7	0	3,575	18th	$2,527,310
Totals	337	4	20	64	5	34,344		$12,790,059

Bobby Hamilton takes his Andy Petree Racing Chevrolet to speed at Lowe's Motor Speedway in May 2002.

Top: Hamilton leads Ricky Craven (No. 32) and Ricky Rudd (No. 28) into the first turn at Martinsville. Two of Hamilton's four career wins have come at that famous Virginia short track. Left: Hamilton looks as though his qualifying attempt wasn't as good as he would have liked at Chicago in July 2001. Right: Hamilton finds a comfortable spot on the pit road wall at Watkins Glen in 2000.

his first track championship there, he began being referred to as a local star. After he won a match race at Nashville in 1988 among Hamilton, Waltrip, Marlin, and Bill Elliott, Waltrip invited Hamilton to qualify his Busch Series car when a schedule conflict dictated that Waltrip arrive late. Hamilton qualified eighth, and Waltrip went on to victory the next day.

In 1990, Hamilton drove in a handful of races for team owner George Bradshaw and won Rookie of the Year honors for the team the following season. He didn't win his first race until he joined Petty Enterprises in 1996, a year in which he finished ninth in the Winston Cup points race. Once that first win came, people began to think of him as having a legitimate shot at victory each week.

Hamilton scored a win for Petty Enterprises at Rockingham in 1997, and followed that with a victory at Martinsville in the spring of 1998 with Morgan-McClure Motorsports. In 2001, Hamilton switched over to Andy Petree Racing. Petree logged many wins as a crew chief with such esteemed drivers as Harry Gant and Dale Earnhardt Sr., and he was the crew chief during Earnhardt's last two Winston Cup championship seasons, in 1993 and 1994. When Hamilton drove the No. 55 Chevrolet to victory at Talladega in April 2001, it was Petree's first as team owner.

Hamilton finished a modest 18th place in the final point standings in 2001, but he was the only driver in Winston Cup competition to be running at the end of all 36 events that season. He also set a career high for earnings that year by collecting $2,527,310, with three top-5 and seven top-10 finishes.

"Winning at Talladega was a big win for me and Andy Petree," Hamilton says. "We knew going into that day he had a great racecar, and everything just came together. Winning in Winston Cup racing is a feeling you just can't describe."

Hamilton enjoys the spoils of victory at Phoenix in 1996 while driving for Petty Enterprises.

GM
Goodwrench
Service
RCR
GM
Goodwrench
Service
NASCAR
Winston Cup

KEVIN HARVICK

29

Born:
December 8, 1975
Bakersfield, California

Height: 5-10

Weight: 175 lbs

Sponsor	**GM Goodwrench**
Make	**Chevrolet**
Crew Chief	**Gil Martin**
Owner	**Richard Childress**

NASCAR Winston Cup Career Statistics

Year	Races	Wins	Top 5s	Top 10s	Poles	Total Points	Final Standing	Winnings
2001	35	2	6	16	0	4,406	9th	$4,302,202
Totals	35	2	6	16	0	4,406		$4,302,202

Only a Hollywood screenwriter could have dreamed up Kevin Harvick's seemingly unbelievable debut in Winston Cup racing in 2001. When the season began, Harvick was just a second-year Busch Series driver for Richard Childress, a year removed from being named Busch Series Rookie of the Year in 2000. By the end of 2001, Harvick was a stock car household name, with two Winston Cup victories, the Winston Cup 2001 Rookie of the Year, and the Busch Series championship under his seatbelt.

Harvick's rise was so surprising because no one could have foreseen the fate of Childress' top driver, legendary seven-time champion Dale Earnhardt. After the black day of February 18, 2001, when Earnhardt was killed on the final lap of the Daytona 500, Childress turned to his new young talent to wheel his Winston Cup cars.

Harvick was quick to make an impact. He scored a photo-finish victory over Jeff Gordon in his third career start, coming at Atlanta only two weeks after Earnhardt's death. Despite the hectic, cross-country schedule, Harvick campaigned in both the Winston Cup and Busch Series divisions simultaneously. The effort paid off. Harvick not only went on to notch a second big-league triumph, at the inaugural Winston Cup event at Chicago, but he also posted several Busch Series races en route to that division's 2001 championship. Counting a NASCAR Craftsman Truck Series event, Harvick entered 70 races in three different series during his remarkable year.

"We were able to accomplish a lot of things, even though it began as such a sad year with the loss of Dale Earnhardt," Harvick says. "I just appreciate Richard Childress for all he's done for me and the confidence he has put in me. I'm not going to let him down. We're gonna continue to win races and championships, hopefully several NASCAR Winston Cup championships before we're done."

Bottom Left: After filling the spot of Dale Earnhardt's No. 3 Chevy for RCR Enterprises, Kevin Harvick's No. 29 Chevy has become well known on the Winston Cup circuit. Above: To the surprise of the racing world, Harvick collected his first Winston Cup win in only the third race of his career, at Atlanta in 2001. The win came three weeks after Dale Earnhardt's death. Bottom Right: Harvick listens intently to his crew as they meet in the garage area at Pocono International Raceway in June 2001.

SIMPSON

DALE JARRETT

88

Born:
November 26, 1956
Conover, North Carolina

Height: 6-2

Weight: 215 lbs

Sponsor	**UPS**
Make	**Ford**
Crew Chief	**Todd Parrott**
Owner	**Robert Yates**

Dale Jarrett finally tamed the treacherous Darlington Raceway in South Carolina with a win in the spring 400-mile event there in 1998. He was following in the footsteps of his famous father, Ned Jarrett, who claimed victory at Darlington in the 1965 Southern 500 and was a two-time NASCAR Grand National champion. The younger Jarrett's journey to stardom was long, however, covering many laps for many team owners.

Dale Jarrett started racing in 1977 at Hickory Motor Speedway in the Limited Sportsman Division before jumping over to the Busch Series when it started in 1982. His Winston Cup career was launched in 1984 with a one-race ride with former driver and team owner Emmanuel Zervackis at Martinsville, Virginia. He started 24th, finished 14th, and collected $1,515 for his first Winston Cup start.

A variety of team owners called on Jarrett to wheel their cars before Cale Yarborough included him in his retirement plans of 1989. Jarrett was to split the schedule with the three-time Winston Cup champion. At the conclusion of that season, however, Yarborough brought in a new driver, and Jarrett found himself without a ride. Fortunately, the search for a new team didn't last long.

When Neil Bonnett, driver of the Wood Brothers Ford, was injured in a crash at Darlington in 1990, Jarrett was tapped to fill the void, presumably for just a race or two. Bonnett's injuries required a lengthy recovery period, however, and Jarrett was put in the driver's seat for the duration of the season.

In August of 1991, Jarrett captured his first career Winston Cup win after battling head-to-head with Davey Allison at Michigan International Speedway, beating the late Alabama driver to the finish line by a foot.

NASCAR Winston Cup Career Statistics

Year	Races	Wins	Top 5s	Top 10s	Poles	Total Points	Final Standing	Winnings
1984	3	0	0	0	0	267	--	$7,345
1986	1	0	0	0	0	76	--	$990
1987	24	0	0	2	0	2,177	25th	$143,405
1988	29	0	0	1	0	2,622	23rd	$118,640
1989	29	0	2	5	0	2,789	24th	$232,317
1990	24	0	1	7	0	2,558	25th	$214,495
1991	29	1	3	8	0	3,124	17th	$444,256
1992	29	0	2	8	0	3,251	19th	$418,648
1993	30	1	13	18	0	4,000	4th	$1,242,394
1994	30	1	4	9	0	3,298	16th	$881,754
1995	31	1	9	14	1	3,584	13th	$1,363,158
1996	31	4	17	21	2	4,568	3rd	$2,985,418
1997	32	7	20	23	3	4,696	2nd	$3,240,542
1998	33	3	19	22	2	4,619	3rd	$4,019,657
1999	34	4	24	29	0	5,262	1st	$6,649,596
2000	34	2	15	24	3	4,684	4th	$5,984,475
2001	36	4	12	19	4	4,612	5th	$5,366,242
Totals	459	28	141	210	15	56,187		$33,313,332

Driving for Robert Yates Racing, Dale Jarrett puts his UPS-sponsored Ford through the paces at Darlington Raceway in March 2002. A victory at Pocono in June was his first of the season.

The next year, Jarrett left Wood Brothers to join the untested Joe Gibbs organization, a move that sparked much criticism. Gibbs had found success with the Washington Redskins of the National Football League, but he came to the racing world at ground zero. Jarrett brought the team to prominence with a victory over Dale Earnhardt in the 1993 Daytona 500.

After Ernie Irvan was gravely injured in an accident during a practice session at Michigan International Speedway in August 1994, Jarrett was again called upon to fill in as an injury replacement. He was released from his contract with Gibbs and took over Irvan's place with the Robert Yates team for the 1995 season.

Despite questions about whether he was experienced enough to take on such a potent ride, Jarrett quickly silenced the critics, winning at Pocono in July and finishing in the top 10 in 14 of 31 races that year. When Irvan miraculously returned for the full season in 1996, Jarrett moved to a second Yates Ford team with crew chief Todd Parrott at the helm. The results were nothing short of dominant.

In 1996, Jarrett won the Daytona 500, the Coca-Cola 600 at Charlotte, the Brickyard 400 at Indianapolis, and the Miller 400 at Brooklyn, Michigan. After a season-long bid for the Winston Cup championship, Jarrett finished a close third behind Terry Labonte and Jeff Gordon.

Three years later, Jarrett finally added that elusive jewel to his crown by claiming the 1999 NASCAR Winston Cup championship with Robert Yates Racing. He finally realized the dream that had been his ever since he was tossing footballs in the Darlington Raceway infield as a child.

"It's hard to put into words how good winning a Winston Cup championship can be," Jarrett said. "I've had a great many supporters who have helped me in various ways throughout my career. Without them, Robert Yates, and the crew members who turn wrenches each week, that championship would only be a dream."

Top: Late in the 2001 season, Jarrett catches a quiet moment in the garage area of Kansas Speedway. Bottom Left: Jarrett calls upon his crew for tires and fuel at Darlington Raceway in September 2000. Bottom Right: Jarrett discusses the performance of the racecar with crew chief Todd Parrott at Daytona in July 1999. Jarrett left Daytona that weekend as the race winner, furthering him on the way to a Winston Cup championship.

Above: Jarrett is all smiles at Pocono Raceway in this photo taken in July 2000. Right: In August of 1999, Jarrett earned one of his most prestigious victories in the Brickyard 400 at Indianapolis Motor Speedway. Below: Jarrett enjoys the moment after collecting his second career Daytona 500 trophy in February 2000. His first Daytona 500 win came in 1993.

DEWALT
RACING
DEWALT
Ford
RACING
GOODYEAR
ROUSH
Racing
DEWALT
NASCAR
Winston Cup

MATT KENSETH

17

Born:
March 10, 1972
Madison, Wisconsin

Height: 5-9

Weight: 152 lbs

Sponsor	**DeWalt**
Make	**Ford**
Crew Chief	**Robbie Reiser**
Owner	**Jack Roush**

NASCAR Winston Cup Career Statistics

Year	Races	Wins	Top 5s	Top 10s	Poles	Total Points	Final Standing	Winnings
1998	1	0	0	1	0	150	--	$42,340
1999	5	0	1	1	0	434	49th	$143,561
2000	34	1	4	11	0	3,711	14th	$2,408,138
2001	36	0	4	9	0	3,982	13th	$2,565,579
Totals	76	1	9	22	0	8,277		$5,159,618

Meet Matt Kenseth back in the garage and you'd say he was a shy, quiet sort. Meet him while he's pushing the throttle on his 3,700-pound Roush Racing Ford out on the oval, and you'll soon see his shy demeanor get blown out the header pipes. Kenseth means business when the green flag falls, and already in his young career he has shown how hungry he is for the wins.

Kenseth's driving career began when his father bought a racecar to drive and had his son maintain it with a few friends who helped on the crew. Once Matt reached his 16th birthday, the car was turned over to him. He progressed to the ARTGO Series and became its youngest winner (besting Winston Cup driver Mark Martin for that honor).

A large part of getting into the Winston Cup arena is getting noticed. When he was a Busch Series standout, Kenseth was tapped to drive for Bill Elliott so that the former Winston Cup champion could attend his father's funeral in September 1998. Kenseth eased Elliott's mind by posting a solid sixth-place finish at Dover, Delaware.

Kenseth was hired by Jack Roush, on Mark Martin's urgent recommendation, for the 2000 Winston Cup season—and the young driver shocked the racing community by winning the Coca-Cola World 600 at Lowe's Motor Speedway in May that year. His 14th-place finish in the points standings was good enough to bring Kenseth the Rookie of the Year award in 2000.

After a winless 2001 campaign, the 30-year-old quickly asserted himself at the front of the pack in 2002. He claimed victory at Rockingham, North Carolina, in the second race of the season, captured another checkered flag at Texas Motor Speedway in April, and added a third trophy to the shelf with a win at Michigan in June.

"Racing stock cars is all I've ever done," Kenseth says. "I just feel fortunate to be running in Winston Cup and winning there. I owe that to Jack Roush."

Top: Matt Kenseth drove his DeWalt-sponsored Ford to a very strong start in 2002. Twelve races into the season, he already had two victories under his belt. Left: Kenseth celebrates his first career NASCAR win in Charlotte's Victory Lane after the 600-mile event there in May 2000. Above: Kenseth often can be seen sporting a smile when things are going right, as he's doing here at Atlanta in 1999.

INTERSTATE
BATTERIES
INTERSTATE
BATTERIES
NASCAR
INTERSTATE
BATTERIES

BOBBY LABONTE 18

Born:
May 8, 1964
Corpus Christi, Texas

Height: 5-9

Weight: 175 lbs

Sponsor	**Interstate Batteries**
Make	**Pontiac**
Crew Chief	**Jimmy Makar**
Owner	**Joe Gibbs**

From all he has accomplished, one might reason that stock car racing is what makes up Texas native Bobby Labonte. Way back in 1984, a shy and rather young Bobby could be found over and underneath the Chevrolets that were being driven by older brother Terry. That year, the elder Labonte captured his first NASCAR Winston Cup championship. While Terry was accepting the trophy and all the checks, Bobby's mental wheels began turning toward putting his own racing career in motion.

Even before Terry's glory days with team owner Billy Hagan, Bobby followed in his brother's footsteps by fielding a quarter-midget racer at the mere age of five. Bobby continued to turn wrenches for Terry through the 1986 season, but the following year he began his own Late Model Sportsman career, where he secured a track championship at Caraway Speedway with 12 victories and 7 pole positions in 23 races.

By 1990, Bobby Labonte's name was stenciled on the rooflines of the Busch Series Chevrolets he had sitting at his Trinity, North Carolina, shop. He finished fourth in the season-long point standings that year, and came back in 1991 to win the NASCAR Busch Series championship. Obviously with

NASCAR Winston Cup Career Statistics

Year	Races	Wins	Top 5s	Top 10s	Poles	Total Points	Final Standing	Winnings
1991	2	0	0	0	0	110	--	$8,350
1993	30	0	0	6	1	3,221	19th	$395,660
1994	31	0	1	2	0	3,038	21st	$550,305
1995	31	3	7	14	2	3,718	10th	$1,413,682
1996	31	1	5	14	4	3,590	11th	$1,475,196
1997	32	1	9	18	3	4,101	7th	$2,217,999
1998	33	2	11	18	3	4,180	6th	$2,980,052
1999	34	5	23	26	5	5,061	2nd	$4,763,615
2000	34	4	19	24	2	5,130	1st	$7,361,386
2001	36	2	9	20	1	4,561	6th	$4,786,779
Totals	294	18	84	142	21	36,710		$25,953,024

Left: Bobby Labonte is at speed in his Joe Gibbs Racing Pontiac at Las Vegas in March 2002.

Right: Labonte enjoys a quiet moment while at Daytona in October 1998.

Above: Labonte enjoys a taste of victory at Pocono International Raceway in 1999. It was one of a career high five wins that season. Below: The intensity can be seen in Labonte's eyes as he awaits the start of a race at Richmond in September 2000.

that kind of success, there was no question Labonte was going to make a career of Winston Cup racing.

Early on, Bobby relied heavily on Terry for advice about which teams to sign with. There were times when Terry saved Bobby from locking himself into teams that weren't championship caliber. By 1993, he found a home with Bill Davis Racing but lost Rookie of the Year honors to future Winston Cup champion Jeff Gordon. Having finished 19th and 21st in the point standings in his first two full seasons, Labonte was happy to take the ride with Joe Gibbs Racing when Dale Jarrett vacated the spot to join Robert Yates in 1995. Labonte won three races that season and set the stage for good things ahead. Since Labonte's union began with the former

coach of the NFL Washington Redskins, record-breaking performances have been the standard for the team from Huntersville, North Carolina, to follow.

Labonte finished a strong second in the 1999 point standings and came back to win his own NASCAR Winston Cup championship in 2000. He collected 4 victories, including a win in the prestigious Brickyard 400, in his title year.

"The great thing about Joe Gibbs Racing is you know what your goal is every year, and that is to give all you've got to win the Winston Cup championship," Labonte says. "What we were able to accomplish in 2000 was really great, and I'm ready to win another championship. I know that's always the focus at Joe Gibbs Racing."

Right: Labonte proudly displays his Winston Cup championship trophy after clinching the title at Homestead, Florida, in November 2000. Below: Labonte's crew services the lime-green Pontiac at Talladega. Labonte is always a threat to win on the superspeedways.

Kellogg's
Racing
CHEEZ-IT
NASCAR
Winston Cup
Series
SIMPSON
DELPHI
GMAC
GOODYEAR
MOTORSPORTS

TERRY LABONTE

5

Born:
November 16, 1956
Corpus Christi, Texas

Height: 5-10

Weight: 165 lbs

Sponsor	**Kellogg's**
Make	**Chevrolet**
Crew Chief	**Jim Long**
Owner	**Rick Hendrick**

Two-time NASCAR Winston Cup champion Terry Labonte may do most of his racing on ovals, but his career has been a real roller-coaster ride. After 23 years of highs and lows, the 45-year-old Texan still challenges the young guns in the drive for another championship.

Labonte's career began when team owner Billy Hagan picked him to drive his Winston Cup cars when Terry was only 22 years old and working as a crew member for Hagan. Labonte took over for Dick May in a race at Dover, Delaware, in September and brought Hagan's No. 92 Chevy home 10th. He also started five events in 1978, finishing in the top 10 three times, including a fourth place at Darlington Raceway in South Carolina, in his first career Winston Cup start. The Texas oilman had found his star. Although seat time was what Labonte needed most, sharing races with May allowed him to keep his rookie status for the following season.

Labonte and Hagan ditched the No. 92 for No. 44 at the start of the 1979 season, and solid, consistent finishes followed. Labonte made 31 starts that year and netted a 10th-place finish in the Winston Cup point standings. He fell just a few spots behind a young driver named Dale Earnhardt in the 1979 Rookie of the Year chase.

NASCAR Winston Cup Career Statistics

Year	Races	Wins	Top 5s	Top 10s	Poles	Total Points	Final Standing	Winnings
1978	5	0	1	3	0	659	39th	$20,545
1979	31	0	2	13	0	3,615	10th	$130,057
1980	31	1	6	16	0	3,766	8th	$215,889
1981	31	0	8	17	2	4,052	4th	$334,987
1982	30	0	17	21	2	4,211	3rd	$363,970
1983	30	1	11	20	3	4,004	5th	$362,790
1984	30	2	17	24	2	4,508	1st	$713,010
1985	28	1	8	17	4	3,683	7th	$694,510
1986	29	1	5	10	1	3,473	12th	$522,235
1987	29	1	13	22	4	4,002	3rd	$825,369
1988	29	1	11	18	1	4,007	4th	$950,781
1989	29	2	9	11	0	3,564	10th	$704,806
1990	29	0	4	9	0	3,371	15th	$450,230
1991	29	0	1	7	1	3,024	18th	$348,898
1992	29	0	4	16	0	3,674	8th	$600,381
1993	30	0	0	10	0	3,280	18th	$531,717
1994	31	3	6	14	0	3,876	7th	$1,125,921
1995	31	3	14	17	1	4,146	6th	$1,558,659
1996	31	2	21	24	4	4,657	1st	$4,030,648
1997	32	1	8	20	0	4,177	6th	$2,270,144
1998	33	1	5	15	0	3,901	9th	$2,054,163
1999	34	1	1	7	0	3,580	12th	$2,475,365
2000	32	0	3	6	1	3,433	17th	$2,239,716
2001	36	0	1	3	0	3,280	23rd	$3,011,901
Totals	709	21	176	340	26	87,943		$26,536,692

During the 2001 Daytona 500, Terry Labonte found himself in a rather intense battle with teammate Jeff Gordon (No. 24) and Rusty Wallace (No. 2).

Labonte's love affair with Darlington continued at the 1980 Southern 500, where he collected his first Winston Cup victory—a win that still ranks among the biggest upsets in the race's history. Leaders David Pearson and Dale Earnhardt hit an oil slick in turn one, caused by Frank Warren's blown engine. Labonte trailed two seconds behind and won the race under caution.

The consistency continued, and in 1984 Labonte gave Hagan his only Winston Cup championship to date. From the outside, it looked as though relations between the champion driver and team owner were at an all-time high, but in the shadows, problems loomed. By 1987, Labonte moved over to Junior Johnson's organization, then one of the top teams on the tour. Limited success came with Johnson through 1989, as was the case with owner Richard Jackson in 1990. A surprise reunion with Hagan came in 1991, and the renewed partnership lasted through 1993. Following his 1984 title run, Labonte claimed only six victories over the next nine seasons, none of them with Jackson or Hagan.

Just as the critics were turning up the assault, saying that Labonte was on the downhill slide—that glory had passed him by—an unexpected turn of events gave new life to his career. Ricky Rudd departed Hendrick Motorsports to start his own Winston Cup organization. Labonte's name surfaced as a possible replacement, and a strong finish at North Wilkesboro in late 1993 convinced team owner Rick Hendrick that Labonte was his man. The union with Hendrick has produced more victories for Labonte (eight) than with any other team owner, and led to a second Winston Cup title in 1996.

In March of 2002, Labonte reflects on another season ahead with Hendrick Motorsports.

The pace slowed down after the second championship, with just one win per season from 1997 to 1999, and a winless 2000 and 2001. But Labonte continues on with Hendrick Motorsports, and the team feels confident in the potential for further success.

"Chemistry between the driver, crew chief, and crew is the key to everything going well," Labonte says. "I think we've got all that back together, so when people ask me about my goals, I tell them I want nothing short of the Winston Cup championship. That's what we're shooting for. You can't go for anything less."

Top: Labonte's Kellogg's-sponsored Chevy makes a scheduled pit stop at Texas Motor Speedway in April 2001. Left: Without the trademark mustache he sported for so many years, Labonte watches carefully as his crew prepares his car at Pocono in 1999. Right: According to Labonte, he couldn't have won at a better track than Texas, his home track, in March 1999.

STERLING MARLIN

40

Born:
June 30, 1957
Columbia, Tennessee

Height: 6-0

Weight: 180 lbs

Sponsor	**Coors Light**
Make	**Dodge**
Crew Chief	**Lee McCall**
Owner	**Chip Ganassi**

The sound of race engines roaring and welders crackling have filled Sterling Marlin's ears for as long as he can remember. Racing is a way of life for Sterling, just as it was for his dad, Clifton "Coo Coo" Marlin. Throughout Sterling's formative years, there was always a stock car of some type sitting in the shed out back. And after nearly three decades of racing in NASCAR, Marlin has never let fame and success taint his easygoing country personality.

At the age of 15, Marlin helped on his dad's pit crew during the summers, and occasionally the underage driver took the wheel of the transporter on the long trips from Columbia, Tennessee, to places like Michigan, Daytona, or Texas. When school was in session, Marlin worked on his dad's cars but stayed home to play football for his high school.

Marlin soon got the chance to fulfill his dream of driving stock cars. With help from his father's Winston Cup sponsor, H. B. Cunningham, the 16-year-old Marlin purchased a 1966 Chevelle to race at the Nashville Speedway. Soon after, in only his third start in a racecar, Marlin relieved his father in a Winston Cup event at Nashville on July 17, 1976. He finished eighth. A year later, he joined his father for his first superspeedway race, running an ARCA (American Race Car Association) car at Talladega.

NASCAR Winston Cup Career Statistics

Year	Races	Wins	Top 5s	Top 10s	Poles	Total Points	Final Standing	Winnings
1976	1	0	0	0	0	76	--	$565
1978	2	0	0	1	0	226	--	$10,170
1979	1	0	0	0	0	123	--	$505
1980	5	0	0	2	0	588	42nd	$29,810
1981	2	0	0	0	0	164	--	$1,955
1982	1	0	0	0	0	94	--	$4,015
1983	30	0	0	1	0	2,980	19th	$143,564
1984	14	0	0	2	0	1,207	37th	$54,355
1985	8	0	0	0	0	721	37th	$31,155
1986	10	0	2	4	0	989	36th	$113,070
1987	29	0	4	8	0	3,386	11th	$306,412
1988	29	0	6	13	0	3,621	10th	$521,464
1989	29	0	4	13	0	3,422	12th	$473,267
1990	29	0	5	10	0	3,387	14th	$369,167
1991	29	0	7	16	2	3,839	7th	$633,690
1992	29	0	6	13	5	3,603	10th	$649,048
1993	30	0	1	8	0	3,355	15th	$628,835
1994	31	1	5	11	1	3,443	14th	$1,127,683
1995	31	3	9	22	1	4,361	3rd	$2,253,502
1996	31	2	5	10	0	3,682	8th	$1,588,425
1997	32	0	2	6	0	2,954	25th	$1,301,370
1998	32	0	0	6	0	3,530	13th	$1,350,161
1999	34	0	2	5	1	3,397	16th	$1,797,416
2000	34	0	1	7	0	3,363	19th	$1,992,301
2001	36	2	12	20	1	4,741	3rd	$4,517,634
Totals	539	8	71	178	11	61,252		$19,899,539

Sterling Marlin's silver Ganassi Racing Dodge ran near the front of the pack in many Winston Cup events in 2002. Here he is shown at Darlington Raceway in March.

Marlin continued on the short tracks and won three consecutive track championships at the Nashville Speedway in 1980, 1981, and 1982. He campaigned the full Winston Cup schedule in 1983 and went on to win Rookie of the Year honors driving for Roger Hamby.

Marlin struggled with various team owners until 1986, when he joined Billy Hagan for four full seasons. Two more seasons with Junior Johnson and one with Stavola Brothers Racing set the stage for his greatest successes, with Morgan-McClure Racing and later with Chip Ganassi.

After nearly 300 starts and nine second-place finishes, Marlin earned his first Winston Cup victory at the 1994 Daytona 500. He defended his Daytona 500 crown the following year, making him only the third driver in history to claim back-to-back Daytona 500 triumphs. Four more victories followed with McClure in 1995 and 1996: two at Talladega, one at Darlington, and a July win at Daytona.

After four winless seasons, Marlin rebounded with new team owner Ganassi in 2001, capturing two checkered flags and the third-place spot in the final points standings. The 2002 campaign started off well, with Marlin taking, and holding, the top spot in the point standings after the first two races on the schedule. He solidified his lead with victories at Las Vegas and Darlington in March, and by finishing in the top 10 in 8 of the first 10 races.

"Stock car racing is all I've ever known," Marlin says. "NASCAR has been real good to me and my family. To win the Daytona 500 back to back is a real dream come true, but of course, anytime you win in Winston Cup it's really great. I know there are some good things to come in my future, maybe even a Winston Cup championship. Still, no matter what happens, I'm always just going to be myself because I really don't think of myself as a celebrity. I'm just Sterling Marlin. Racing is all I've ever done."

Marlin is all smiles as he strolls down pit road at Martinsville in October 2001.

Above: At Atlanta Motor Speedway in March 2001, Marlin does battle with teammate Casey Atwood. Below: Marlin's victory at Michigan in August 2001 was the first for Dodge in NASCAR Winston Cup competition since 1977. Right: Though he is often quiet when he's outside of his racecar, Marlin makes a lot of noise on the racetracks of Winston Cup.

MARK MARTIN

6

Born:
January 9, 1959
Batesville, Arkansas

Height: 5-6

Weight: 135 lbs

Sponsor	**Pfizer/Viagra**
Make	**Ford**
Crew Chief	**Ben Leslie**
Owner	**Jack Roush**

Mark Martin's game plan is usually pretty simple: win the race. If the win doesn't come, a strong finish in the top five will have to do.

Even when he was racing as a teenager back in the early 1970s, Martin was no different. If there was a race to win, he had the talent and equipment to mix it up with the very best. He battled veteran drivers such as Bobby Allison, Dick Trickle, and Jim Sauter for American Speed Association (ASA) victories. Long before he was of legal age, Martin mastered the tracks of the Midwest better than some with twice the experience. He racked up hundreds of wins in addition to four ASA championships.

Martin took his winning ways to the Winston Cup arena in 1981, using a couple of his own Buick Regals. He scored two pole positions that year, one top 5, and one top 10. The strong start grabbed the attention of more than one team owner, but Martin again fielded his own team for the full schedule in 1982. He came up short to Geoff Bodine in the Rookie of the Year race, and fell short to the bank for the many dollars spent. His only chance to survive was as a hired gun for an owner hoping to make it big.

What followed was bittersweet. Team owner J. D. Stacy hired Martin in 1983 for what was to be a full schedule of racing. However, after only seven races, including a third-place finish at Darlington, Stacy fired Martin, a move that remains a mystery to some.

For the remainder of the 1983 season and over the next few years, Martin picked up rides wherever he could, first with D. K. Ulrich, then in five events with J Gunderman in 1986, and one event for Roger Hamby in 1987. It was a tough existence. Then came the break of a lifetime.

NASCAR Winston Cup Career Statistics

Year	Races	Wins	Top 5s	Top 10s	Poles	Total Points	Final Standing	Winnings
1981	5	0	1	2	2	615	42nd	$13,950
1982	30	0	2	8	0	3,181	14th	$126,655
1983	16	0	1	3	0	1,621	30th	$99,655
1986	5	0	0	0	0	488	48th	$20,515
1987	1	0	0	0	0	46	--	$3,550
1988	29	0	3	10	1	3,142	15th	$223,630
1989	29	1	14	18	6	4,053	3rd	$1,019,250
1990	29	3	16	23	3	4,404	2nd	$1,302,958
1991	29	1	14	17	5	3,914	6th	$1,039,991
1992	29	2	10	17	1	3,887	6th	$1,000,571
1993	30	5	12	19	5	4,150	3rd	$1,657,662
1994	31	2	15	20	1	4,250	2nd	$1,628,906
1995	31	4	13	22	4	4,320	4th	$1,893,519
1996	31	0	14	23	4	4,278	5th	$1,887,396
1997	32	4	16	24	3	4,681	3rd	$2,532,484
1998	33	7	22	26	3	4,964	2nd	$4,309,006
1999	34	2	19	26	1	4,943	3rd	$3,509,744
2000	34	1	13	20	0	4,410	8th	$3,098,874
2001	36	0	3	15	2	4,095	12th	$3,797,006
Totals	494	32	188	293	41	65,442		$29,165,322

Mark Martin hits the concrete at Las Vegas Motor Speedway in March 2002. A third-place finish there helped put Martin in the top 5 in the point standings.

Automotive engineer Jack Roush was forming a Winston Cup team and needed an experienced driver. Martin got word that a search was on, and he convinced Roush to hire him. Money was never a consideration. His only desire was to be back with an established team in Winston Cup competition.

At the start of the 1988 Winston Cup season, Roush recognized Martin's burning desire to win and hired him over a long list of applicants. The first victory came on October 22, 1989, at North Carolina Motor Speedway in Rockingham. Since then, Martin and Roush have scored 17 more victories and 29 pole positions, and established themselves as winners in the NASCAR Busch Series.

In 1995, Martin scored four victories, one each coming on the short track at North Wilkesboro, North Carolina, the intermediate-sized Charlotte Motor Speedway, the road course at Watkins Glen, New York, and the superspeedway at Talladega, Alabama. Although the wins have dwindled in recent years, the 32 career victories (through 2001) put Martin in rare company on the NASCAR circuit.

Above: Martin is helmeted and ready to do battle before the start of an event at North Carolina Speedway in Rockingham. Right: Martin is in deep discussion with team owner Jack Roush prior to the start of the 500-mile event at Talladega Superspeedway in October 2001.

Top Left: Martin proved in October 1998 that he could still get the job done. Here he stands as the winner of the 500-mile event at Charlotte. Top Right: Martin has driven the No. 6 Ford for most of his Winston Cup career, and the pit crew has been crucial to the team's success. Bottom Left: Martin addresses fans and the media prior to the start of the Daytona 500 in February 1998. Bottom Right: Martin sits idle in the garage area at Las Vegas in 1998, reflecting on what he has to do to get a win there. A day later, he enjoyed the spoils of victory.

At the start of the 2002 season, owner Jack Roush made some radical changes by switching Martin's crew with Kurt Busch's, hoping to give both teams new blood to get them to winning status.

"The move of crews between the two teams is a good concept," Martin said. "Sometimes change is needed to move forward and I'm sure both me and Kurt [Busch] will find the success we're looking for in 2002 and beyond."

DODGE
NASCAR
Winston Cup
Series

JEREMY MAYFIELD

19

Born:
May 27, 1969
Owensboro, Kentucky

Height: 6-0

Weight: 190 lbs

Sponsor	**Dodge Dealers**
Make	**Dodge**
Crew Chief	**Sammy Johns**
Owner	**Ray Evernham**

There must be something in the water around Owensboro, Kentucky. Jeremy Mayfield, driver of the Evernham Motorsports Dodge, joins a long list of drivers who hail from that Southern town, including the three Green brothers (David, Mark, and Jeff) and the Waltrips (Michael and three-time champ Darrell). Whatever the reason, Mayfield certainly has the talent to make big things happen racing against his fellow Owensboro natives.

Like so many southern stock car drivers, Mayfield began his career as a go-kart racer and eventually moved through the ranks of Street Stocks, Sportsman, and Late Models. Winning the 1987 Rookie of the Year award at Kentucky Motor Speedway brought Mayfield one step closer to his dream of driving and winning at the NASCAR Winston Cup

NASCAR Winston Cup Career Statistics

Year	Races	Wins	Top 5s	Top 10s	Poles	Total Points	Final Standing	Winnings
1993	1	0	0	0	0	76	--	$4,830
1994	20	0	0	0	0	1,673	37th	$226,265
1995	27	0	0	1	0	2,637	31st	$436,805
1996	30	0	2	2	1	2,721	26th	$592,853
1997	32	0	3	8	0	3,547	13th	$1,067,203
1998	33	1	12	16	1	4,157	7th	$2,332,034
1999	34	0	5	12	0	3,743	11th	$2,125,227
2000	32	2	6	12	4	3,307	24th	$2,169,251
2001	28	0	5	7	0	2,651	35th	$2,682,603
Totals	237	3	33	58	6	24,512		$11,637,071

Jeremy Mayfield at speed on the concrete racing surface at Dover, Delaware, in June 2002.

The Penske Racing team goes to work on Mayfield's Ford during a pit stop at Texas Motor Speedway in 2001. Mayfield drove for Penske before making the switch to Evernham's team.

level. He became a regular on the ARCA circuit in 1993 and had finishes good enough to earn him his second rookie honor.

Mayfield finally made his Winston Cup debut at Charlotte in October 1993, driving for team owner Earl Sadler. Sadler had fielded cars for several notable up-and-coming drivers—including the late Davey Allison—so Mayfield appeared to be on the right path. He wheeled Sadler cars for four races in 1994, and T. W. Taylor also brought Mayfield on for four events that year. Then NASCAR legend Cale Yarborough called and asked for Mayfield's services. Many predicted it would be a prosperous marriage, but after 12 races in 1994 and a full season in 1995, the wins simply didn't come.

Late in the season in 1996, owners Yarborough and Michael Kranefuss swapped drivers. Mayfield went to work for Kranefuss while John Andretti went over to Yarborough's team. (Andretti won the 400-mile event at Daytona for Yarborough in 1997.)

After Kranefuss joined with racing legend Roger Penske, Mayfield had the best ride of his career. He scored wins at Pocono, Pennsylvania, in 1998 and 2000, as well as a win at California in 2000. In addition, there were pole positions at Darlington, Dover, Rockingham, Talladega, and Texas.

Despite the two wins, not all was well in 2000, as things slowly unraveled for the Penske-Mayfield partnership. When Mayfield's car was found to be too low after the California win, it seemed to mark the beginning of the end. Even though Mayfield had nothing to do with the height of the car, there was discord within the team. Finally, after additive was added to his gas tank by a crew member just before Mayfield's pole position run at Talladega, the end was all but written.

Apparently, both owner and driver wanted and needed a change after the tumultuous

2000 campaign. Mayfield finally got his wish the day after the inaugural event at Kansas Speedway in September 2001, when Penske Racing released Mayfield from his contract. From that day until the start of Speedweek 2002 that kicked off the new season, Mayfield sat on the sidelines waiting for a new ride. Finally, Evernham Motorsports came along, and a new relationship was formed.

"This team has a great deal of potential and I'm ready to go racing," Mayfield says. "All it takes is some time to sit back and watch to get a driver fired up about driving again. And it definitely feels good to be back driving again."

Above: Mayfield anticipates the start of the Winston Cup event at Las Vegas in March 2001. Left: Mayfield waves to the crowd during pre-race ceremonies prior to the start of the 600-mile event at Charlotte in May 2000.

UAW
DELPHI
UAW-DELPHI

JERRY NADEAU

25

Born:
September 9, 1970
Danbury, Connecticut

Height: 5-6

Weight: 150 lbs

Sponsor	**UAW**
Make	**Chevrolet**
Crew Chief	**Tony Furr**
Owner	**Rick Hendrick**

NASCAR Winston Cup Career Statistics

Year	Races	Wins	Top 5s	Top 10s	Poles	Total Points	Final Standing	Winnings
1997	5	0	0	0	0	287	54th	$118,545
1998	30	0	0	0	0	2,121	36th	$804,867
1999	34	0	1	2	0	2,686	34th	$1,370,229
2000	34	1	3	5	0	3,273	20th	$2,164,778
2001	36	0	4	10	0	3,675	17th	$2,507,827
Totals	139	1	8	17	0	12,042		$6,966,246

Long before becoming the driver of "Pappa" Joe Hendrick's No. 25 Chevrolets, Jerry Nadeau got his start as a master of karting. He knows karts so well that he won 10 World Karting Association and International Karting Foundation championships between 1984 and 1990. Just for fun, he entered a go-kart event in St. Petersburg, Russia, in 1992 and finished second—not a bad run, considering the race was on ice.

Stock cars had always grabbed Nadeau's attention, and he attended some driving schools, including that of road race ace Skip Barber. Nadeau won Rookie of the Year in Barber's Racing Series and scored eight wins in 1993. From 1993 through 1995, he won nine races in the series. Nadeau finished sixth overall in the 1996 Formula Opel European Series, the highest finish ever by an American.

When Nadeau entered the world of NASCAR Winston Cup racing in 1997, he did so on a limited schedule with team owner Richard Jackson. From the moment he rolled through the garage gate, virtually everyone's eyes were fixed on the kid from Danbury, Connecticut. He routinely mixed it up with the veterans at the front of the pack and did a masterful job in the process.

In 1998, former champion Bill Elliott tapped Nadeau to wheel his cars. Although little success came from that venture, team owner Rick Hendrick saw Nadeau's raw talent. He moved to Hendrick's organization in 2000 and won the season-ending Winston Cup event at Atlanta Motor Speedway. He came close to another win there at the end of 2001, but an empty fuel tank on the last lap took the win away.

"I still say we have great potential with this Hendrick Motorsports team," Nadeau says. "I'm sure we'll be winning at places other than just Atlanta real soon."

Above: Jerry Nadeau's UAW Chevrolet makes the rounds at Las Vegas in March 2002.

Right: Nadeau stands in Victory Lane at Atlanta Motor Speedway in November 2000—his only Winston Cup victory to date.

BELL

JOE NEMECHEK

26

Born:
September 26, 1963
Lakeland, Florida

Height: 5-9

Weight: 185 lbs

Sponsor	**Kmart**
Make	**Ford**
Crew Chief	**Donnie Wingo**
Owner	**Haas/Carter**

For Joe Nemechek, if it goes fast, then you can race it. From the time Joe and his brother John were old enough to reach the pedals on their bicycles, they dreamed of becoming stars in NASCAR. They both wanted their names to be listed alongside those of such heroes as David Pearson, Richard Petty, Cale Yarborough, and of course, Bobby Allison—another driver who liked to race anything that could go like spit. Sadly, at the young age of 27, John Nemechek lost his life in an accident during a NASCAR Craftsman Truck Series event in March 1997.

From an early age, Joe Nemechek has had the word "champion" associated with his name. He began racing motocross at age 13, winning more than 300 trophies in six years, before entering the realm of short-track events in his native Florida in 1987.

Never one to do anything halfway, Nemechek won Rookie of the Year honors and championships in three straight years: the Southeastern Mini Stock Series in 1987, the U.S.A.R. Series in 1988, and the All-Pro Series in 1989. He went on to take the NASCAR Busch Series championship in 1992 before officially joining the Winston Cup ranks in 1993. To date, he is a two-time winner in Winston Cup and has won nearly $10 million in earnings.

Nemechek's success has come in cars owned by himself as well as those of Larry Hedrick, Felix Sabates, and Andy Petree. On September 19, 1999, he won for Sabates at New Hampshire, and in 2001, he drove Petree's car to victory at North Carolina Motor Speedway in Rockingham.

"Driving in NASCAR is, without a doubt, a huge dream come true," Nemechek says. "There might someday be a Winston Cup championship in the future. I think there will be."

NASCAR Winston Cup Career Statistics

Year	Races	Wins	Top 5s	Top 10s	Poles	Total Points	Final Standing	Winnings
1993	5	0	0	0	0	389	44th	$56,580
1994	29	0	1	3	0	2,673	27th	$389,565
1995	29	0	1	4	0	2,742	28th	$428,925
1996	29	0	0	2	0	2,391	34th	$666,247
1997	30	0	0	3	2	2,754	28th	$732,194
1998	32	0	1	4	0	2,897	26th	$1,343,991
1999	34	1	1	3	3	2,956	30th	$1,634,946
2000	34	0	3	9	1	3,534	15th	$2,105,042
2001	31	1	1	4	0	2,994	28th	$2,510,723
Totals	253	2	8	32	6	23,330		$9,868,213

Above: Joe Nemechek brings the Andy Petree Racing Chevrolet up to speed at New Hampshire in July 2001.

Left: Nemechek celebrates a surprise win at New Hampshire Speedway in September 1999.

ALLTEL
Ford
RACING

RYAN NEWMAN

12

Born:
December 8, 1977
South Bend, Indiana

Height: 5-11

Weight: 207 lbs

Sponsor	**Alltel**
Make	**Ford**
Crew Chief	**Matt Borland**
Owner	**Roger Penske**

NASCAR Winston Cup Career Statistics

Year	Races	Wins	Top 5s	Top 10s	Poles	Total Points	Final Standing	Winnings
2000	1	0	0	0	0	40	--	$37,825
2001	7	0	2	2	1	652	49th	$465,276
Totals	8	0	2	2	1	692		$503,101

Ever since Rick Hendrick discovered Jeff Gordon within the open-wheel Sprint Car ranks, other team owners have scoured the Sprint grids for potential future champions. Tony Stewart, Casey Atwood, Casey Mears in the NASCAR Busch Series, and Jason Leffler in the NASCAR Truck Series, are just a few of those who have been lifted from open-wheel racing. When team owners Roger Penske, Don Miller, and Rusty Wallace went out looking for new talent, they discovered Ryan Newman, a 24-year-old open-wheel star who is already in the Quarter Midget Hall of Fame.

Newman graduated from Purdue University with a degree in Vehicular Structural Engineering, something that might come in handy when setting up some of the Winston Cup machines. He pulled off wins in ARCA (Automobile Racing Club of America) competition at Pocono, Kentucky Speedway, and Charlotte. He was also victorious in all three USAC divisions: midgets, sprint cars, and the Silver Bullet Series.

Newman competed in both the Winston Cup and Busch Series in 2001, and his impact on the scene was almost immediate. In only his third career Winston Cup start, he scored a pole position in the 600-mile event at Charlotte. In seven starts that season, Newman kept his Penske Racing Ford up front on several occasions. He grabbed a fifth-place finish at Michigan in June, and topped that with a second-place running, behind Jeff Gordon, at Kansas Speedway's inaugural race in September. Newman and his team are full of confidence for a full season on the circuit.

"I'm extremely thankful to Roger Penske for this great opportunity," Newman says. "This is a top-flight operation and I'm sure we'll have a lot of success together in the coming years."

Right: Focus and determination put Ryan Newman alongside some savvy veterans during his rookie campaign on the Winston Cup Circuit. Below: The young Newman is already making a name for himself in his Penske Racing Ford. At Darlington in March 2002 he earned a fifth-place finish.

STEVE
PARK
PENNZOIL RACING

STEVE PARK

1

Born:
August 23, 1967
East Northport, New York

Height: 6-2

Weight: 190 lbs

Sponsor	**Pennzoil**
Make	**Chevrolet**
Crew Chief	**Paul Andrews**
Owner	**DEI**

When Dale Earnhardt was looking for a driver to wheel his Chevrolets in the Busch Series for the team he was developing, Dale Earnhardt Inc., he needed a hot shoe who was young and hungry to win. He placed his confidence in Steve Park, a driver who went on to show his famous employer that he could win in Winston Cup competition as well. Park began racing in the northeastern United States, following in the footsteps of his father, Bob Park, a winning modified driver in the region for many years. Now Bob Park drives modifieds in the New York area in cars owned by his famous son, Steve.

NASCAR Winston Cup Career Statistics

Year	Races	Wins	Top 5s	Top 10s	Poles	Total Points	Final Standing	Winnings
1997	5	0	0	0	0	326	51st	$74,480
1998	17	0	0	0	0	1,322	42nd	$487,265
1999	34	0	0	5	0	3,481	14th	$1,767,690
2000	34	1	6	13	2	3,934	11th	$2,283,629
2001	24	1	5	12	0	2,859	32nd	$2,385,971
Totals	114	2	11	30	2	11,922		$6,999,035

Steve Park's yellow-and-black No. 1 machine is familiar to NASCAR fans. Here he passes the grandstands at Martinsville Speedway in April 2002.

From the ARCA division to the NASCAR Featherlite Modified Series in 1995, Steve Park put together a program good enough to finish second in the season-long points battle. When he won three times and took Rookie of the Year honors in Earnhardt's car in 1997, he was already being talked about as a promising Winston Cup star.

Since entering the Winston Cup arena in 1998, Park's career has been one of feast or famine. Before he could even get his career going, he crashed during a practice session at Atlanta Motor Speedway and suffered a severely broken leg that caused him to miss 15 of the scheduled 34 events. He came back to finish 11th at Michigan Speedway in August of that year, and again at Dover Downs a month later.

In 2000, Park broke into Victory Lane by winning at Watkins Glen, the track he considers his home track. One of Park's most special moments was having Earnhardt greet him in Victory Lane after he stood on top of his yellow-and-black Chevrolet.

A year later, despite the tragic death of his team owner and mentor, Park seemed to be on the fast track to success. Just one week after Earnhardt lost his life on the final lap of the Daytona 500, Park scored a photo-finish victory over Bobby Labonte at

Park ponders the race ahead at Dover Downs in June 2000.

Rockingham. He followed that up with 11 more top-10 finishes, including second places at Darlington, Texas, and Dover Downs.

Twenty-four races into the season, Park was sitting in 10th place in the Winston Cup point standings when he was involved in a freak accident during a Busch Series event. Crew members within the sport speculate that the steering wheel on Park's Chevrolet was not properly attached by the standard pin that secured it to the steering column. The wheel came off in his hands under caution, and without control of the car, he was T-boned in the driver's side by Larry Foyt, who was moving up to his proper starting position on the inside line as a lapped car.

Park suffered head injuries in the crash, requiring many months of slow recovery. He finally climbed back into his No. 1 Chevy five races into the 2002 season, trying to regain his previous form with each passing week.

"We were wide open and our lap times show we weren't holding anything back," Park said after a test at Atlanta Motor Speedway. "I know I can race now. I just want to make sure that when I come back I want to be in a position to win. Before the accident, I went 200 miles per hour behind the wheel of a racecar. Now I've been going 200 miles per hour with rehab and everything to get back there."

Above: Suited up and ready for action, Park is focused behind the wheel of his DEI Chevrolet Monte Carlo at Darlington in September 2000. Below Left: The DEI crew works fast to keep Park's ride running smoothly. Below Right: Park studies the winding road course at Watkins Glen. In August 2000, he scored his first career Winston Cup victory there.

Hot Wheels
Racing

KYLE PETTY

45

Born:
June 2, 1960
Trinity, North Carolina

Height: 6-2

Weight: 195 lbs

Sponsor	**Sprint**
Make	**Dodge**
Crew Chief	**Steven Lane**
Owner	**Petty Enterprises**

When your last name is Petty and your father is known as "The King" of stock car racing, your career is pretty much pre-ordained. Even before he ever drove a racecar, Kyle Petty was being touted as a star of the future. He was the talk of racing circles at home and abroad. Surely he would be a chip off the old block, they said. A born success.

As a child, Kyle saw stock car racing as nothing more than his father's profession. The cars in the nearby shop were shiny blue with painted numbers on their doors, set up to be turned left around short tracks and superspeedways. He was surrounded by the sounds of air grinders hitting metal and engines screaming on the dynamometer.

Kyle at first resisted the seemingly predetermined path to the oval track during his adventurous and trouble-filled teenage years, but he eventually turned his energies toward his destiny. To become a Winston Cup racer was a tough but reasonable goal for any young driver. To meet the high expectations that come with bearing the Petty name, under the intense scrutiny of the press and public, was a much different story.

At the start of Speedweek in 1979, Petty came to Daytona International Speedway with a Dodge Magnum, a discarded Winston Cup machine his father had used with no success the year before. Although it had a heavy box-like design, the car was perfect for the younger Petty, who entered it in ARCA competition.

Miraculously, Kyle met the media expectations right off the bat. He won the ARCA 200 in his first outing on a closed course. For a brief time, he was the only undefeated stock car driver in America.

His career launched, a total of 169 races passed before Petty found Victory Lane in Winston Cup competition. It came in 1986, at the short track in Richmond,

NASCAR Winston Cup Career Statistics

Year	Races	Wins	Top 5s	Top 10s	Poles	Total Points	Final Standing	Winnings
1979	5	0	0	1	0	559	37th	$10,810
1980	15	0	0	6	0	1,690	28th	$36,350
1981	31	0	1	10	0	3,335	12th	$112,289
1982	29	0	2	4	0	3,024	15th	$120,730
1983	30	0	0	2	0	3,261	13th	$157,820
1984	30	0	1	6	0	3,159	16th	$324,555
1985	28	0	7	12	0	3,523	9th	$296,367
1986	29	1	4	14	0	3,537	10th	$403,242
1987	29	1	6	14	0	3,732	7th	$544,437
1988	29	0	2	8	0	3,296	13th	$377,092
1989	19	0	1	5	0	2,099	30th	$117,022
1990	29	1	2	14	2	3,501	11th	$746,326
1991	18	1	2	4	2	2,078	31st	$413,727
1992	29	2	9	17	3	3,945	5th	$1,107,063
1993	30	1	9	15	1	3,860	5th	$914,662
1994	31	0	2	7	0	3,339	15th	$806,332
1995	30	1	1	5	0	2,638	30th	$698,875
1996	28	0	0	2	0	2,696	27th	$689,041
1997	32	0	2	9	0	3,455	15th	$984,314
1998	33	0	0	2	0	2,675	30th	$1,287,731
1999	32	0	0	9	0	3,103	26th	$1,278,953
2000	19	0	0	1	0	1,441	41st	$894,911
2001	24	0	0	0	0	1,673	43rd	$1,008,919
Totals	609	8	51	167	8	65,619		$13,331,568

Kyle Petty at speed at Darlington in September 2001. The one-groove racetrack isn't one of Petty's favorites. He once jokingly suggested it be filled with water and minnows for fishing.

Petty deep in thought at Pocono Raceway in July 2001—his eyes fixed on the future of his famous family's race team.

Virginia, with the Wood Brothers team. The win established him as the first third-generation driver to win a Winston Cup race. His grandfather, Lee, won his first race in 1949, and his father, Richard, first stood on the top spot in 1960. Kyle notched another win in 1987 at the Coca-Cola 600, his first superspeedway triumph.

Six more wins followed with team owner Felix Sabates, but the Cuban transplant and the North Carolina country boy parted ways in 1996 after eight seasons together. They had become as close as father and son, but the results on the track didn't warrant another year together.

Petty elected to field his own cars in 1997 and 1998, meeting only limited success. In 1999, he reopened Petty Enterprises, partly to field cars for his son Adam in the Busch Series and, eventually, Winston Cup. That dream came to a tragic end when young Adam was killed in a single-car accident during a practice session at New Hampshire International Raceway on May 12, 2000. Since his son's death, Petty has campaigned the colors, sponsors, and number Adam used in Busch Series competition and his lone Winston Cup start at Texas Motor Speedway two weeks before his death. It is in memory of his son that Kyle hopes to bring Petty Enterprises back to winning form.

"I just want to win races and win championships," Petty says. "You want to run competitively and have shots at winning each week. I don't look at a lot of statistics and never have. My father never did. It's amazing that he won as much as he did, but that wasn't the point. The point was to win races, and the championships followed."

Above: In the garage area at Daytona in 1998, Petty stands in front of one of the Petty Enterprises toolboxes that carries the familiar Petty decals. Below: Just four months after his son, Adam, lost his life in a crash during a Busch Series practice session, Petty began driving his son's racecar in Adam's sponsors' colors. Here, Petty gets ready for an event at Darlington in September 2000.

SHAWNA ROBINSON

49

Born:
November 30, 1964
Des Moines, Iowa

Height: 5-6

Weight: 110 lbs

Sponsor	**BAM Motorsports**
Make	**Dodge**
Crew Chief	**Eddie Sharp**
Owner	**Elizabeth Morgenthau**

NASCAR Winston Cup Career Statistics

Year	Races	Wins	Top 5s	Top 10s	Poles	Total Points	Final Standing	Winnings
2001	1	0	0	0	0	61	--	35,190
Totals	1	0	0	0	0	61		35,190

Shawna Robinson, driver of the BAM Motorsports Dodge, displays many talents. There is no question she can drive a racecar—she routinely out-qualifies some of her male counterparts who have been on the circuit for years. Though many have questioned her ability to succeed in the pressure-filled NASCAR arena, her way of silencing those critics is to take to the racetrack and put a good run on the scoring pylon.

As the rare female on the stock car racing scene, Robinson's career has been a long sequence of "firsts." In 1988, she became the first woman to win a Touring Series event in 40 years of NASCAR. A year later, she was the first woman to win a pole position in the NASCAR Goody's Dash Series. In 1994, Robinson won the pole position for the Busch Light 300 at Atlanta Motor Speedway, posting a track record speed of 174.33 miles per hour. She finished sixth in the ARCA season point standings, making her the first and (to date) only woman in history to make the top 10 in points in any national oval-track motorsports series. In

Above: Shown here at Daytona in February 2000, Shawna Robinson has been well accepted as the only woman on the NASCAR Winston Cup circuit. Left: Robinson is leaving her mark on the NASCAR scene. Her performance at Atlanta in March 2002 was her third finish in four races.

2000, she became the first woman to complete a full oval-track racing schedule in the ARCA Series.

On June 10, 2001, Robinson started in 32nd position at the Kmart 400 at Michigan International Speedway, making her the first female driver to start a Winston Cup race in 12 years. In 1989, Patti Moise started an Oldsmobile owned by racing legend Buddy Baker at Watkins Glen, but she did not complete the event due to a mechanical failure. When Robinson finished the 2001 race, in the 34th spot, she was the first woman to make it to the finish line at a NASCAR event since Janet Guthrie did it in 1980.

Now, Robinson must look to the NASCAR Winston Cup Series as her new home, and many people are wildly cheering her on. She may someday be the first woman to win a Winston Cup race—or maybe even a championship.

"Teamwork has been a big part of the success we have shared in the one race we have worked together," Robinson says. "The No. 49 BAM Racing team has overcome a few setbacks, and we still finished in the top 25 at Daytona. That says a lot about the guys. We have come into this with a winning mentality, and I know the best is yet to come.

"When it comes to driving the racecar, the racecar doesn't know which gender is pushing the throttle. I see a lot of good things happening in our future. I don't think being male or female has anything to do with it. It's a person's talent behind the wheel that counts."

Above: One can see that Robinson is very serious about her racing. Right: Robinson battles Ken Schrader for position at Michigan International Speedway in June 2001. She finished 34th but became the first woman since Janet Guthrie in 1980 to finish a Winston Cup event.

Robinson suits up in her full-face helmet before an ARCA event at Michigan in June 2000.

Winston Cup
Series
Coca-Cola
SIMPSON
Ford

RICKY RUDD

28

Born:
September 12, 1956
Chesapeake, Virginia

Height: 5-8

Weight: 160 lbs

Sponsor	**Texaco/Havoline**
Make	**Ford**
Crew Chief	**Michael McSwain**
Owner	**Robert Yates**

Ricky Rudd's youthful face has been seen in Victory Lane at least once every season for 17 years, making him one of the most consistent drivers on the Winston Cup circuit. Along with his wins have come many pole positions and more than $24 million in career earnings.

Rudd began racing motocross and go-karts at a very early age but didn't drive a stock car until he first sat down in a Winston Cup ride in 1975 at age 18. He took four starts that year with Bill Champion, and one top-10 finish foretold Rudd's potential. In 1976, he started four more events, this time in cars fielded by his father, Al Rudd Sr., and reeled off another top-10 finish—a hint of the consistency that would mark his lengthy career. With his family-owned team, Rudd tackled the majority of the schedule in 1977, competing in 25 events, and earned Rookie of the Year honors after finishing 17th in the point standings that season.

Rudd came back to start in 13 races in 1978, garnering results sufficient to land a ride with longtime team owner Junie Donlavey for the full schedule in 1979. He scored two third-place finishes and two fifths in 1979, earning him nearly $150,000. Overall, it was a good learning season for Rudd.

In 1980, back with the Rudd family operation for 13 events, Ricky found himself in a make-or-break situation. Money was running out fast, but one good race could get him noticed by the better-financed teams on the circuit, providing perhaps his only chance to remain an active driver. That October, Rudd entered the National 500 at Charlotte Motor Speedway in a year-old car and qualified on the outside front row. By race's end, Rudd was fourth, finishing behind legends Dale Earnhardt, Cale Yarborough, and Buddy Baker. As hoped, the impressive run caught the notice of several veteran team owners.

NASCAR Winston Cup Career Statistics

Year	Races	Wins	Top 5s	Top 10s	Poles	Total Points	Final Standing	Winnings
1975	4	0	0	1	0	431	53rd	$4,345
1976	4	0	0	1	0	407	56th	$7,525
1977	25	0	1	10	0	2,810	17th	$68,448
1978	13	0	0	4	0	1,264	32nd	$49,610
1979	28	0	4	17	0	3,642	9th	$146,302
1980	13	0	1	3	0	1,319	32nd	$50,500
1981	31	0	14	17	3	3,991	6th	$381,968
1982	30	0	6	13	2	3,542	9th	$201,130
1983	30	2	7	14	4	3,693	9th	$257,585
1984	30	1	7	16	4	3,918	7th	$476,602
1985	28	1	13	19	0	3,857	6th	$512,441
1986	29	2	11	17	1	3,823	5th	$671,548
1987	29	2	10	13	0	3,742	6th	$653,508
1988	29	1	6	11	2	3,547	11th	$410,954
1989	29	1	7	15	0	3,608	8th	$534,824
1990	29	1	8	15	2	3,601	7th	$573,650
1991	29	1	9	17	1	4,092	2nd	$1,093,765
1992	29	1	9	18	1	3,735	7th	$793,903
1993	30	1	9	14	0	3,644	10th	$752,562
1994	31	1	6	15	1	4,050	5th	$1,044,441
1995	31	1	10	16	2	3,734	9th	$1,337,703
1996	31	1	5	16	0	3,845	6th	$1,503,025
1997	32	2	6	11	0	3,330	17th	$1,975,981
1998	33	1	1	5	0	3,131	22nd	$1,602,895
1999	34	0	3	5	1	2,922	31st	$1,632,011
2000	34	0	12	19	2	4,575	5th	$2,974,970
2001	36	2	14	22	1	4,706	4th	$4,878,027
Totals	731	22	179	344	27	88,959		$24,590,223

Ricky Rudd has had great success in the famous No. 28 Havoline Ford driven by such notable drivers as Davey Allison, Ernie Irvan, Dale Jarrett, and Kenny Irwin. Here, Rudd is shown taking the car around the bends at Bristol in March 2002.

Rudd signed with Digard Racing for the 1981 season, replacing Darrell Waltrip, who vacated the high-profile ride to drive for Junior Johnson. Even though the results from the Digard-Rudd union weren't overly impressive, there were definite signs of promise.

Rudd switched to the Richard Childress team in 1982, and his first Winston Cup victory came the following year at the Budweiser 400 in Riverside, California. Over the next few years, Rudd won six races driving for Bud Moore, two more with Kenny Bernstein, and captured four wins and a second-place finish in the 1991 Winston Cup point championship with Rick Hendrick. Since then, he has scored more victories with his own team and with Robert Yates, a longtime friend he joined at the start of the 2000 season.

Since entering the Winston Cup circuit, Rudd's name has surfaced each season as a driver who is a constant threat for victory. With the Yates organization, Rudd has had longtime members of the press believing that he will return to championship status.

"I spent six seasons trying to make a winning team out of my own organization, but that just didn't work," Rudd says. "Now I'm winning races with Robert and enjoying my career again. Robert has a powerhouse organization, and I'm honored to be driving for him. My goal is to get at least one championship before I retire, and I feel like I can get that done with Robert's team."

Above: Rudd wears the Texaco Havoline star proudly. Right: Rudd battles Rusty Wallace (in the No. 2 Miller Lite car) down the stretch at the 2002 Daytona 500.

Above: Rudd shares a light moment with fellow driver Tony Stewart before an event at Pocono Raceway. Left: Rudd is focused behind the wheel of his Robert Yates Racing Ford at Rockingham in February 2002.

Motorcraft
QUALITY PARTS
Racing
wood brothers
Stuart, Va.

ELLIOTT SADLER 21

Born:
April 30, 1975
Emporia, Virginia

Height: 6-2

Weight: 195 lbs

Sponsor	**Motorcraft**
Make	**Ford**
Crew Chief	**Pat Tryson**
Owner	**Len and Eddie Wood**

NASCAR Winston Cup Career Statistics

Year	Races	Wins	Top 5s	Top 10s	Poles	Total Points	Final Standing	Winnings
1998	2	0	0	0	0	128	--	$45,325
1999	34	0	0	1	0	3,191	24th	$1,589,221
2000	33	0	0	1	0	2,762	29th	$1,578,356
2001	36	1	2	2	0	3,471	20th	$2,683,225
Totals	105	1	2	4	0	9,552		$5,896,127

Elliott Sadler seemingly has enjoyed going fast since a rather young age. He began racing go-karts at age seven. By the time he turned to stocks cars at the age of 18, he had compiled the same winning record as Richard Petty. While the legendary Petty amassed 200 victories on the Winston Cup tour, Sadler matched the feat in the go-kart ranks.

Before long, the urge to take his racing to a higher level brought Sadler to NASCAR's Busch Series. In 76 starts in the series, Sadler logged five victories and 12 top fives. His standout abilities caught the attention of brothers Len and Eddie Wood in 1999. Like Sadler, the Wood brothers hail from Virginia, and the three have felt a kinship since the moment they first drove through a speedway gate as driver and team owners.

Wood Brothers Racing and the number they campaign are storied legends in NASCAR. The team has enjoyed great success over the years with a "Who's Who" of drivers that has included names like Marvin Panch, Curtis Turner, and David Pearson. The Wood Brothers still apply the famous number 21 on the doors of their fleet of Fords.

Sadler showed early in his Winston Cup career that he has the talent to follow in the footsteps of those drivers of the past. He quickly repaid the Wood brothers' confidence in him with a win at Bristol Motor Speedway in April 2001.

"This race team has won a lot of races over the years [97 victories since 1953], and I want to keep up that tradition for them," Sadler says. "We won at Bristol, and I'm sure another one is right around the corner. This team is awesome and can hold their own. I'm proud to be with this race team."

Above: Behind the controls of his racecar, Elliott Sadler prepares for the start of an event at Dover International Speedway in June 2000. Right: Sadler excelled to a new level with his first career victory at Bristol Motor Speedway in March 2001. Below: Driving for Wood Brothers Racing, Sadler puts his No. 21 Ford to the test at Darlington Raceway in March 2001.

Pedigree
SIMPSON
NASCAR
Winston Cup
Series
Valvoline
Pedigree
GOODYEAR

KEN SCHRADER

36

Born:
May 29, 1955
Fenton, Missouri

Height: 5-9

Weight: 200 lbs

Sponsor	**M&M's**
Make	**Pontiac**
Crew Chief	**Newt Moore**
Owner	**MB2 Motorsports**

Don't look now, but longtime NASCAR racer Ken Schrader isn't exactly ready to sit on the front porch anytime soon. He still has some wins in him, and they're ready to burst out. Looking back on Schrader's life, that's really all he's ever known.

Since he was a toddler, Ken Schrader knew his life would be going around in circles. When Ken was three years old, his father, Bill Schrader, a former racer himself, placed a truck axle in the ground and secured it upright with concrete. After the foundation had dried, the elder Schrader attached one end of a 20-foot cable to the pole and the other end to a go-kart. Young Kenny would strap himself in, push the throttle, and turn left in a circle until he ran out of gas. Over and over, he ran his kart—at least until the tires were nearly burned off the wheels or one of numerous clutches failed. And a new career was born.

Schrader raced go-karts at age 3, quarter midgets by 5, and motorcycles by the time he was 10 years old. In 1971, he won his first track championship in Hobby Class cars at the ripe old age of 16.

NASCAR Winston Cup Career Statistics

Year	Races	Wins	Top 5s	Top 10s	Poles	Total Points	Final Standing	Winnings
1984	5	0	0	0	0	449	53rd	$16,425
1985	28	0	0	3	0	3,024	16th	$211,523
1986	29	0	0	4	0	3,052	16th	$235,904
1987	29	0	1	10	1	3,405	10th	$375,918
1988	29	1	4	17	2	3,858	5th	$631,544
1989	29	1	10	14	4	3,786	5th	$1,039,441
1990	29	0	7	14	3	3,572	10th	$769,934
1991	29	2	10	18	0	3,690	9th	$772,439
1992	29	0	4	11	1	3,404	17th	$639,679
1993	30	0	9	15	6	3,715	9th	$952,748
1994	31	0	9	18	0	4,060	4th	$1,171,062
1995	31	0	2	10	1	3,221	17th	$886,566
1996	31	0	3	10	0	3,540	12th	$1,089,603
1997	32	0	2	8	2	3,576	10th	$1,355,292
1998	33	0	3	11	2	3,675	12th	$1,887,399
1999	34	0	0	6	1	3,479	15th	$1,939,147
2000	34	0	0	2	0	3,398	18th	$1,711,476
2001	36	0	0	5	0	3,485	19th	$2,418,181
Totals	528	4	64	176	23	60,389		$18,104,281

Ken Schrader battles for position in his MB2 Motorsports Pontiac with Michael Waltrip (No. 15) at Darlington Raceway in September 2001. Darlington is considered one of the toughest racetracks on the circuit.

Schrader sports his familiar headgear while waiting for the start of a race at Richmond in May 2000.

As a kid, Schrader would walk the 8 miles down the road to his father's short track, Lake Hill Speedway, in Valley Park, Missouri. He practiced flagging the racecars as they came through the gate, or stood in his front yard and gave them the green flag as they passed by.

The itch to compete in NASCAR just had to be scratched by the early 1980s. In 1984, Schrader joined Elmo Langley, a veteran Winston Cup competitor who had vacated his driver's seat to give way to more youthful talent. The following year, Schrader joined Junie Donlavey and took home the Winston Cup Rookie of the Year. He remained with Donlavoy for throo full coacons, with solid results. He scored 17 top-10 finishes in those three years, and ended up with 10th place in the point standings in his final year with Donlavey in 1987.

While working miracles with limited financing, Schrader caught the eye of team owner Rick Hendrick. The positive results of the new partnership were evident immediately, as Schrader won his first Winston Cup race in 1988 at Talladega, and finished fifth in the standings in 1988 and again in 1989. During his nine-year relationship with Hendrick, Schrader grabbed four victories and 14 pole positions in 267 starts. He also won the Busch Clash in 1989 and 1990, and took the pole position for the Daytona 500 three years running in 1988, 1989, and 1990.

Near the end of 1996, Schrader and Hendrick parted company, each citing the need to try their hands elsewhere. Andy Petree, a former crew chief for owners Leo Jackson and Richard Childress, hired Schrader after purchasing Jackson's team.

Schrader spent three years with Petree but couldn't buy a win. At the start of the 2000 season, he moved over to join the Pontiac operation of Nelson Bowers. No wins have come as of yet, but the team continues to show progress.

"I've enjoyed a great career, both on the short tracks and with NASCAR Winston Cup racing," Schrader says. "Man, I like to race more than anything else I do. I've done nothing else in my life. Racing is really important to me. I just want to win more races."

Above Left: Schrader is known around Winston Cup circles for sharing a laugh or two with fellow competitors. Above Right: A fixture in Winston Cup racing since 1987, Schrader is all smiles in February 1998. Right: The MB2 Motorsports Pontiac that Schrader drives for 36 races per season sports one of the most unique paint schemes in racing.

NASCAR
Winston Cup
Series

MIKE SKINNER

4

Born:
June 6, 1957
Susanville, California

Height: 6-0

Weight: 200 lbs

Sponsor	**Kodak**
Make	**Chevrolet**
Crew Chief	**Scott Eggleston**
Owner	**Morgan-McClure**

The Morgan-McClure Chevrolets driven by Mike Skinner are a Winston Cup win waiting to happen. From 1986 to 1994, Skinner competed in 10 Winston Cup events with various fledgling team owners, hoping to put up a good-enough showing to attract a major team and sponsor. He found out that being discovered doesn't happen overnight. But people were watching.

Skinner had little more than a pocketful of ambition when he first pursued the Winston Cup circuit. Letting his desire to break into Winston Cup racing be known, Skinner landed rides with non-factory supported teams owned by Thee Dixon and Jimmy Means. Even though the wins didn't come, powerhouse team owners such as Richard Childress and Junior Johnson could see his potential.

Finally, in 1995, Skinner got an unexpected phone call from Childress, owner of RCR Enterprises, who offered him the chance to drive a NASCAR Craftsman Truck

NASCAR Winston Cup Career Statistics

Year	Races	Wins	Top 5s	Top 10s	Poles	Total Points	Final Standing	Winnings
1986	3	0	0	0	0	264	--	$4,255
1990	1	0	0	0	0	58	--	$2,825
1991	2	0	0	0	0	110	--	$8,505
1992	2	0	0	0	0	173	--	$13,450
1993	1	0	0	0	0	58	--	$5,180
1994	1	0	0	0	0	70	--	$9,550
1996	5	0	0	0	0	529	47th	$65,850
1997	31	0	0	3	2	2,669	30th	$900,569
1998	30	0	4	9	0	3,153	21st	$1,518,901
1999	34	0	5	14	2	4,003	10th	$2,499,877
2000	34	0	1	11	1	3,898	12th	$2,205,320
2001	23	0	0	1	0	2,029	40th	$1,921,186
Totals	167	0	10	38	5	17,014		$9,155,468

With a new sponsor in 2002, Mike Skinner is looking to head for the front of the pack.

in the series' inaugural season. At first, Skinner wasn't really interested, noting that Winston Cup was where he wanted to be. Childress counseled patience, and with some persuasion, the two came to an agreement to field a truck team. Skinner rewarded Childress' faith in him with the series championship that year. Things were moving ahead faster than at any point in his career.

Skinner continued on the truck circuit in 1996 until he found himself wheeling a Winston Cup machine for RCR Enterprises in August. The ride belonged to Childress' primary driver, Dale Earnhardt, who had been injured in a crash at Talladega the week before. For Earnhardt, what hurt more than the injuries was the fact that he couldn't defend his title in the Brickyard 400 at Indianapolis Motor Speedway, which he had won the year before. Earnhardt started the event in 12th position, but he reluctantly slid out from behind the wheel and handed the reins over to his replacement. Skinner brought the car home 15th.

The following year, as promised, Skinner was given a Winston Cup ride of his own. He ran the full season and earned the Rookie

Top: During a break in the action, Skinner sits on the driver's side door of his racecar, waiting for the signal to begin practice. Left: Skinner gets service from his crew during a pit stop at Darlington Raceway in September 2001.

of the Year award. He took the pole at both points races at Daytona International Speedway, including the season-opening Daytona 500.

The next four-plus years saw some good runs, but Skinner could only win on foreign soil, gaining victory in exhibition races in Suzuka, Japan, in 1997 and in Motegi, Japan, in 1998. His 10th-place finish in the 1999 point standings is his highest finish to date.

The 2001 Winston Cup season dealt Skinner several injuries, enough that he resigned from RCR Enterprises late in the year to undergo knee surgery. He came back strong in 2002 with Morgan-McClure, a winning team that needed a solid shot in the arm. The partnership with owner Larry McClure just may provide Skinner with the missing ingredient to finally bring him that elusive first official win.

"You keep looking for the right chemistry until you find it," Skinner says. "Hopefully for our benefit and Larry [McClure] and everybody at Morgan-McClure Racing, we've found it this time. Our main objective is to become competitive again. A team with this much depth should have a chance to run well."

Top: Skinner's intensity can be seen on his face during a break at Pocono Raceway in July 2000. Bottom Left: Skinner is slightly hidden from view once readied behind the controls of his racecar. Here, he is set to start an event at Darlington in March 1999. Bottom Right: Skinner enjoys a comment from an RCR Enterprises crew member via the radio earpieces he has in place before race time at Talladega Superspeedway in April 1999.

TARGET
CHIP GANASSI
RACING
FELIX SABATES

JIMMY SPENCER

41

Born:
February 15, 1957
Berwick, Pennsylvania

Height: 6-0

Weight: 230 lbs

Sponsor	**Target**
Make	**Dodge**
Crew Chief	**Doug Randolph**
Owner	**Chip Ganassi**

Ever since Jimmy Spencer arrived on the Winston Cup scene, he has been known to stir things up, especially when a long and uneventful race really needs stirring. The native of Berwick, Pennsylvania, knows nothing but pushing the throttle to the floor and cranking the wheel hard left.

In 1986 and 1987, Spencer showed he was serious about winning when he collected back-to-back Winston modified championships. He progressed the next season into the NASCAR Busch Series, and he continues to compete in that series along with his Winston Cup efforts. In his first Winston Cup experience, Spencer ran 17 races in 1989 for legend-turned-owner Buddy Baker. There, too, Spencer showed great promise but just couldn't break into the winner's circle. Team owners Rod Osterland and Travis Carter also enjoyed good finishes with Spencer in 1990 and 1991, respectively.

NASCAR Winston Cup Career Statistics

Year	Races	Wins	Top 5s	Top 10s	Poles	Total Points	Final Standing	Winnings
1989	17	0	0	3	0	1,570	34th	$121,065
1990	26	0	0	2	0	2,579	24th	$219,775
1991	29	0	1	6	0	2,790	25th	$283,620
1992	12	0	3	3	0	1,284	33rd	$186,085
1993	30	0	5	10	0	3,496	12th	$686,026
1994	29	2	3	4	1	2,613	29th	$479,235
1995	29	0	0	4	0	2,809	26th	$507,210
1996	31	0	2	9	0	3,476	15th	$1,090,876
1997	32	0	1	4	0	3,079	20th	$1,073,779
1998	31	0	3	8	0	3,464	14th	$1,741,012
1999	34	0	2	4	0	3,312	20th	$1,752,299
2000	34	0	2	5	0	3,188	22nd	$1,936,762
2001	36	0	3	8	2	3,782	16th	$2,669,638
Totals	370	2	25	70	3	37,442		$12,747,382

Jimmy Spencer is known as "Mr. Excitement" for how he performs on the racetrack and what he says off the track. Here he speeds along the track at Dover in June 2002.

Above: Spencer pulls his Ford into the pits for tires and fuel at Talladega in April 2000. Right: Spencer looks to be studying the happenings in the garage area in this July 1999 photograph at Pocono Raceway, a facility he calls his home track.

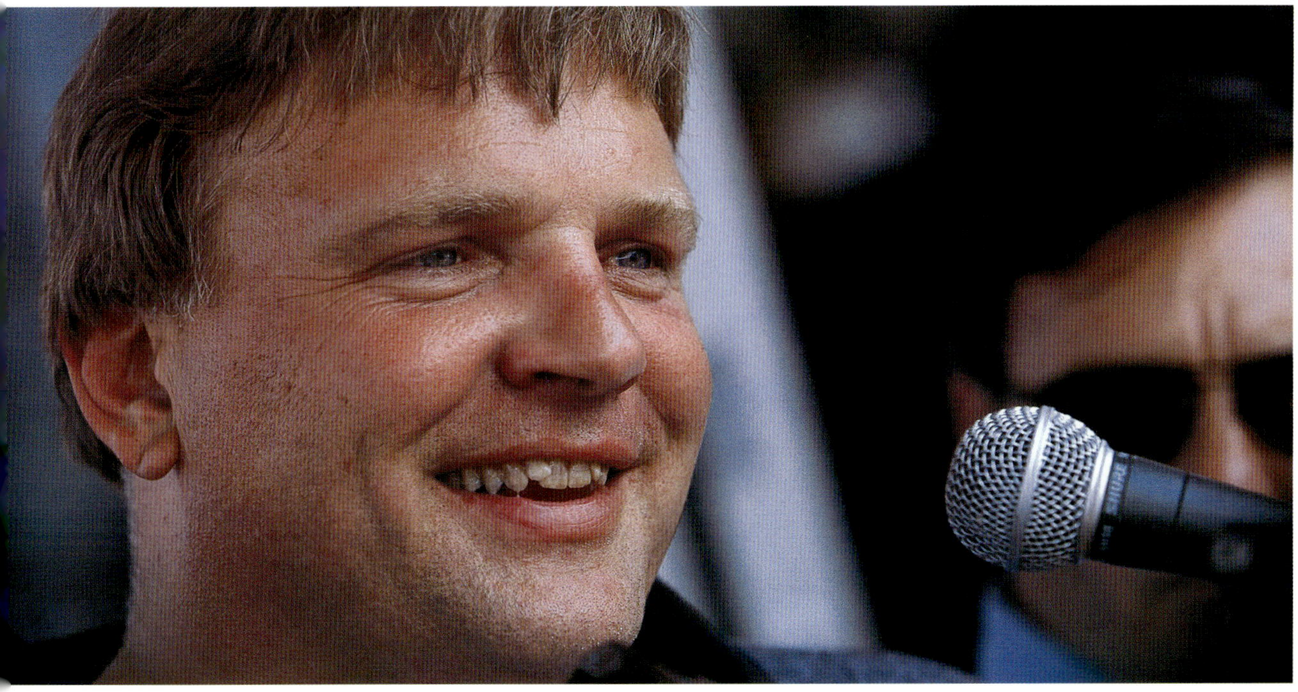

Left: Spencer seemingly always has the media around him when he's not behind the controls of his racecar. Here, he answers questions at Michigan Speedway in August 1998. Below: Spencer is the last driver on the circuit to still wear the open-face helmet, as is shown in this October 2001 photograph at Martinsville Speedway.

Because of Spencer's strong efforts in the series, another legendary former driver, Bobby Allison, invited him to join his team for the Winston Cup Series in 1992. Over a two-year period, Spencer had 13 top-10 finishes in Allison's Fords, including a high of second place at the Winston 500 at Talladega in 1993.

Then came Junior Johnson, a man known for winning races and championships. He won 50 races on his own as a driver and twice that many with a veritable "Who's Who" of drivers wheeling his cars, from Cale Yarborough and Neil Bonnett to Terry Labonte and Geoffrey Bodine, to name a few. Johnson's desire for drivers to push the button, and the fact that Spencer knew no other way to race, made for a perfect pair. At the start of the 1994 Winston Cup season, Spencer immediately showed his strength at the Daytona 500, and then went on to win the Pepsi 400 there in July and the DieHard 500 at Talladega three weeks later, notching victories at the two foremost restrictor-plate tracks.

Spencer elected to return to the cars fielded by Travis Carter in 1995, but found little success. Still, the driver and team owner remained together until the end of the 2001 season.

For 2002 Spencer hooked up with Chip Ganassi and Felix Sabates, driving Dodges for the first time in his career. His first season with the new owners and new cars began on a dismal note. Because he was not able to post a speed or finish high enough in one of the two 125-mile qualifying events at Daytona International Speedway, he could not start the season-opening Daytona 500. Nevertheless, Spencer feels he has made the right move.

"I'm glad I made the change," Spencer said in *NASCAR Winston Cup Scene*. "I feel like if I hadn't taken that ride [with Ganassi], I would have retired with Travis. I don't know where we can go, to tell you the truth, but it's going to be pretty good."

THE HOME DEPOT
Coca-Cola

TONY STEWART 20

Born:
May 20, 1971
Rushville, Indiana

Height: 5-9

Weight: 170 lbs

Sponsor	**Home Depot**
Make	**Pontiac**
Crew Chief	**Greg Zipadelli**
Owner	**Joe Gibbs**

NASCAR Winston Cup Career Statistics

Year	Races	Wins	Top 5s	Top 10s	Poles	Total Points	Final Standing	Winnings
1999	34	3	12	21	2	4,774	4th	$3,190,149
2000	34	6	12	23	2	4,570	6th	$3,642,348
2001	36	3	15	22	0	4,763	2nd	$4,941,463
Totals	104	12	39	66	4	14,107		$11,773,960

When Tony Stewart arrived in the NASCAR Winston Cup arena to drive Pontiacs for team owner Joe Gibbs, most everyone billed him as a likely instant winner. The Indiana native had already spent many years winning races in the Open Wheel Sprint Car ranks as well as in the most elite of open-wheel arenas, the Indianapolis 500. With such tremendous talent established so early on, the gates of Victory Lane would most certainly not be padlocked long while he was around.

Stewart exceeded expectations and began his Winston Cup portfolio by breaking the record for wins by a rookie and winning the 1999 NASCAR Winston Cup Rookie of the Year. His first career victory came in his 25th start, at Richmond International Raceway in Virginia. By season's end, Stewart and his team were clicking well enough to win back-to-back races at Phoenix, Arizona, and Homestead, Florida.

Perhaps Stewart's most impressive accomplishment of 1999 was racing in both the Coca-Cola World 600 at Charlotte and

Above: Tony Stewart is set and ready for action as he awaits the start of the race at Rockingham in October 2000. That year, Stewart finished sixth in the Winston Cup point standings.

Left: Stewart's orange-and-white Pontiac is becoming one of the most recognized rides on the Winston Cup circuit.

Above: Stewart shares a laugh with Joe Gibbs Racing teammate Bobby Labonte in the garage area at Darlington in 2000. Left: Stewart shows his anger toward Kenny Irwin after the two made contact on the track at Martinsville, Virginia, in March 1999.

the Indianapolis 500 on the same day—and go on to post respectable finishes in both events. After an exhaustive 1,100 miles of high-speed magic, he finished fourth in the 600 at Charlotte Motor Speedway and ninth in the 500 at Indianapolis Motor Speedway. Stewart joined Robbie Gordon and John Andretti as the only drivers ever to compete in both events on the same day, but Stewart's efforts produced the best results.

In 2000, many looked to Stewart to pull off the rare accomplishment of winning a Winston Cup championship the very next year after capturing rookie honors. Only one other man, the late and legendary Dale Earnhardt, has achieved such a feat. Unfortunately, Stewart got off to a slow start in his sophomore season, ultimately finishing a respectable sixth in points, while teammate Bobby Labonte captured his first Winston Cup championship.

The next year, Tony Stewart enjoyed his best season to date. He started 2001 off with a victory in the Bud Shoot-Out, a special non-points event for pole-position winners. In June, he was a winner on the road course at Sears Point, California. He followed that performance with another victory at Richmond and also pulled off a win at the demanding high-banked short track of Bristol Motor Speedway. In the end, he finished second to Jeff Gordon in the overall championship hunt after coming on strong at the end when others suffered mechanical failures.

For the second time in his career, Stewart attempted the Charlotte-Indy double duty in 2001. He again finished strong, coming in sixth in the 500 and third in the 600 at Charlotte. Although he passed on the mixed doubleheader in 2002, many continue to view Stewart as a strong championship contender. Wins at Atlanta and Richmond early in 2002 reasserted his place among the leaders.

"If we're going to win the championship, we're going to have to have consistency," Stewart says. "Anyone who's won the Winston Cup championship has done so because they were consistently better than everyone else. That means no DNFs [Did Not Finish] and no riding around in 35th place."

Top: Stewart leads the field at Lowe's Motor Speedway in October 2000. Even though he has yet to win at the 1.5-mile speedway, some of his best finishes have come at the Charlotte track. Above: Number 1 again! Stewart posted two wins early in the 2002 season, including the MBNA America 500 at Atlanta Motor Speedway in March. Left: Stewart makes a pit stop at Las Vegas in March 2002 en route to recording another top-5 finish.

NASCAR
Winston Cup
Series
CHAMPION
SIMPSON
Coca-Cola

KENNY WALLACE

1

Born:
August 23, 1963
Fenton, Missouri

Height: 5-11

Weight: 180 lbs

Sponsor	**Pennzoil**
Make	**Chevrolet**
Crew Chief	**Paul Andrews**
Owner	**DEI**

NASCAR Winston Cup Career Statistics

Year	Races	Wins	Top 5s	Top 10s	Poles	Total Points	Final Standing	Winnings
1990	1	0	0	0	0	85	--	$96,050
1991	5	0	0	0	0	412	44th	$58,325
1993	30	0	0	3	0	2,893	23rd	$330,325
1994	12	0	1	3	0	1,413	40th	$235,005
1995	11	0	0	0	0	875	42nd	$151,700
1996	30	0	0	2	0	2,694	28th	$457,665
1997	31	0	0	2	2	2,462	33rd	$939,001
1998	31	0	0	7	0	2,615	31st	$1,019,861
1999	34	0	3	5	0	3,210	22nd	$1,416,208
2000	34	0	1	1	0	2,877	26th	$1,723,966
2001	24	0	1	2	1	2,054	39th	$1,507,922
Totals	243	0	6	25	3	21,590		$7,936,028

Kenny Wallace may still be looking for that elusive first victory on the NASCAR Winston Cup circuit, but the laughs come easy for this would-be stand-up comic. While filling in as an interim driver for Dale Earnhardt Inc. in Steve Park's Chevrolets, Wallace has nothing but jokes to tell in the garage areas on the 36-race schedule. But when it comes to standing on the throttle in any of the Winston Cup or Busch Series cars he drives, it's no laughing matter.

The native of Fenton, Missouri, and younger brother of 1989 Winston Cup champion Rusty Wallace has proven time and time again that he can take a racecar to the front of the field on a Sunday afternoon. In 2002, he split his time between the top two series while Park recuperated from head injuries suffered during a Busch Series event at Darlington Raceway in September 2001.

For 11 seasons, Wallace has shown some impressive moves on the racetrack, and he continues to impress his fellow drivers. No matter the power of the machines he is asked to drive, Wallace seems to have the magic to log acceptable finishes. Known as "Herman" in the garage area for the name he uses on the two-way radio during races, Wallace is always creating a stir with his hardy laugh and infectious grin.

"As far as I'm concerned, NASCAR racing is the best racing there is in the world," Wallace says. "I have so much fun driving these things, and one day we're gonna get some wins in the wins column—I promise you that!"

Above: Kenny Wallace sports shades while waiting for the start of the event at Darlington in 2001. Left: Wallace fights off Jimmy Spencer in the Target-sponsored Dodge at Rockingham in February 2002.

RUSTY WALLACE 2

Born:
August 14, 1956
Fenton, Missouri

Height: 6-0

Weight: 185 lbs

Sponsor	**Miller Lite**
Make	**Ford**
Crew Chief	**Bill Wilburn**
Owner	**Roger Penske**

When a bushy-haired Rusty Wallace brought a Roger Penske–owned Chevrolet to Atlanta Motor Speedway on March 16, 1980, the young Missourian wasn't supposed to have much of a chance. After all, he was a rookie competing in his first Winston Cup event. But Wallace made the most of his ride that day, mixing it up with the veterans of the sport and making it look easy. Wallace was leading with 29 laps to go when Dale Earnhardt passed him for the win. Wallace held on for second place, and the sensational debut was an indication of things to come.

Wallace won rookie honors in USAC competition in 1979 and was the 1983 ASA champion. Wallace established himself throughout the Midwest as a strong threat to win anywhere he raced, and he entered select Cup races, hungry for a ride in the big show. In his first full season in NASCAR Winston Cup racing, Wallace teamed with owner Cliff Stewart to become the 1984 Rookie of the Year. His first victory came in the 76th start of his career, on April 6, 1986, at Bristol Motor Speedway.

Within just two years Wallace was contending for the championship, finishing as runner-up for the 1988 Winston Cup title to Bill Elliott by only 24 points. A year later,

NASCAR Winston Cup Career Statistics

Year	Races	Wins	Top 5s	Top 10s	Poles	Total Points	Final Standing	Winnings
1980	2	0	1	1	0	291	--	$22,760
1981	4	0	0	1	0	399	--	$12,895
1982	3	0	0	0	0	186	--	$7,655
1983	0	0	0	0	0	0	--	$1,100
1984	30	0	2	4	0	3,316	14th	$195,927
1985	28	0	2	8	0	2,867	19th	$233,670
1986	29	2	4	16	0	3,757	6th	$557,354
1987	29	2	9	16	1	3,818	5th	$690,652
1988	29	6	19	23	2	4,464	2nd	$1,411,567
1989	29	6	13	20	4	4,176	1st	$2,247,950
1990	29	2	9	16	2	3,676	6th	$954,129
1991	29	2	9	14	2	3,582	10th	$502,073
1992	29	1	5	12	1	3,556	13th	$657,925
1993	30	10	19	21	3	4,446	2nd	$1,702,154
1994	31	8	17	20	2	4,207	3rd	$1,914,072
1995	31	2	15	19	0	4,240	5th	$1,642,837
1996	31	5	8	18	0	3,717	7th	$1,665,315
1997	32	1	8	12	1	3,598	9th	$1,705,625
1998	33	1	15	21	4	4,501	4th	$2,667,889
1999	34	1	7	16	4	4,155	8th	$2,454,050
2000	34	4	12	20	9	4,544	7th	$3,621,468
2001	36	1	8	14	0	4,481	7th	$4,788,652
Totals	562	54	182	292	35	71,977		$29,657,719

Always a threat to win in his Penske Racing Ford, Rusty Wallace shows his muscle at Bristol in March 2002. It was one of several top-10 finishes for the Miller Lite car.

after a season-long battle with Earnhardt, Wallace was crowned the 1989 NASCAR Winston Cup champion with team owner Raymond Beadle, inching out The Intimidator by 12 points.

After an 11-year separation, Wallace joined up again with Roger Penske in 1991, now as an established winner. His best years in the victory category came in 1993 and 1994, when he logged 18 wins in 61 starts over the two seasons. At the end of the 1996 season, Wallace won the inaugural Suzuka Thunder 100, a special non-points event held in Suzuka, Japan.

Wallace is undoubtedly one of the hottest stars in Winston Cup racing, having won at least one race in every season since 1986. He constantly demands more and more perfection from his crew. With Roger Penske, a longtime motorsports magnate who has enjoyed much success in Indy car racing, Wallace knows the chemistry is always there for success. Over a 17-year period, Wallace has collected 54 Winston Cup victories, 36 of them with Penske's organization. Now, all Wallace wants is more wins and at least one more Winston Cup championship before he someday turns his attention to other business ventures.

"As far as I'm concerned, you have to think championship all the time," Wallace says. "But the wins and top fives have to come to get that championship. You have to be consistently in the top five every week. If you can do that, you can win championships. That's what we work for each time we unload our rocket off the truck. Aside from that, I wanted to be remembered by the fans as a guy who pushed the gas and was a consistent winner."

Top Left: Wallace enjoys the cheers he receives at Bristol Motor Speedway in August 1998. He often admits that Bristol is one of his favorite tracks. Top Right: Wallace speeds along the concrete at Rockingham early in the 2002 season. Right: Wallace is in a familiar pose behind the controls of the Penske Racing Ford at New Hampshire in 1997.

Above: Wallace makes a pit stop at Sears Point Raceway in California, a track where he earned victories in 1990 and again in 1996. Left: Wallace enjoys a spare moment in the garage area at Dover in June 2001. The 1989 Winston Cup Champion would love to have another taste of the title before he retires. Right: Wallace raises his arms in victory after taking the checkered flag at Bristol Motor Speedway in March 2000. It was Wallace's 53rd career win.

Winston Cup
Series
76
BIG

DARRELL WALTRIP

66

Born:
February 5, 1947
Owensboro, Kentucky

Height: 6-1

Weight: 190 lbs

Sponsor	**Kmart**
Make	**Ford**
Crew Chief	**Larry Carter**
Owner	**Travis Carter & Carl Haas**

When Darrell Waltrip shelved his helmet for the last time in 1999, having won 84 races over a 27-year career, a seat much slower was waiting for him in front of the camera. Of all the past champions who have retired to the broadcast booth, Waltrip is one of the most colorful and best-loved personalities.

When he emerged on the NASCAR scene in 1972, Waltrip was just what the young sport of Winston Cup racing needed—a Kentucky gentleman whose words were as smooth as the liquor produced in the state's mountain region. Vibrant and flamboyant, he was never one to keep his thoughts to himself. He was known to find the empty microphone, tap its cover to get the crowd's attention, shout out predictions, then back them up with action. Those actions—a controversial rub here, a questionable driving style there—ensured that he (and NASCAR racing) remained in the limelight.

At times, fans expressed their dislike for Waltrip, but such behavior never unnerved him—negative attention was better than none. Waltrip's first victory came on May 10, 1975, in his home state of Tennessee using a car built by the prestigious Holman-Moody racing operation. Later that year, he got his chance with a prominent ride, that of the struggling but well-financed Digard Racing Company. Waltrip was heavily criticized for making the move, but once again he backed up his words with actions, and made the team a winner 26 times over the next five and a half years.

A contract dispute with Digard owners Bill and Jim Gardner in 1980 threatened to curtail Waltrip's career. He paid big money, $325,000, to settle the dispute out of court.

The grass, and the money, were definitely greener on the other side of the fence with new owner Junior Johnson, whom he

NASCAR Winston Cup Career Statistics

Year	Races	Wins	Top 5s	Top 10s	Poles	Total Points	Final Standing	Winnings
1972	5	0	1	3	0	--	--	$8,615
1973	19	0	1	5	0	--	28th	$33,466
1974	16	0	7	11	1	--	19th	$57,690
1975	28	2	11	14	2	3,462	7th	$100,192
1976	30	1	10	12	3	3,505	8th	$191,501
1977	30	6	16	24	3	4,498	4th	$276,312
1978	30	6	19	20	2	4,362	3rd	$343,367
1979	31	7	19	22	5	4,819	2nd	$523,691
1980	31	5	16	17	5	4,234	5th	$382,138
1981	31	12	21	25	11	4,880	1st	$693,342
1982	30	12	17	20	7	4,489	1st	$873,118
1983	30	6	22	25	7	4,620	2nd	$824,858
1984	30	7	13	20	4	4,230	5th	$703,876
1985	28	3	18	21	4	4,292	1st	$1,318,735
1986	29	3	21	22	1	4,180	2nd	$1,099,735
1987	29	1	6	16	0	3,916	4th	$511,768
1988	29	2	10	14	2	3,764	7th	$731,659
1989	29	6	14	18	0	3,971	4th	$1,323,079
1990	23	0	5	12	0	3,013	20th	$530,420
1991	29	2	5	17	0	3,711	8th	$604,854
1992	29	3	10	13	1	3,659	9th	$876,492
1993	30	0	4	10	0	3,479	13th	$746,646
1994	31	0	4	13	0	3,688	9th	$835,680
1995	31	0	4	8	1	3,078	19th	$850,632
1996	31	0	0	2	0	2,657	29th	$740,185
1997	31	0	1	4	0	2,942	26th	$958,679
1998	33	0	1	2	0	2,957	24th	$1,056,475
1999	27	0	0	0	0	2,158	37th	$973,133
2000	29	0	0	0	0	1,981	36th	$1,246,280
Totals	809	84	276	390	59	96,545		$19,416,618

Darrell Waltrip drove a chrome-plated-style paint scheme in "The Winston" special non-points event held at Charlotte in May 2000.

Above: Three-time champion Darrell Waltrip makes a pit stop during his final road course event at Watkins Glen, New York, in August 2000. Right: Waltrip shares a smile as he waits for the start of the race at Watkins Glen. Below: Waltrip looks a bit worried behind the wheel of his Travis Carter Racing Ford at Indianapolis in August 2000. After qualifying, Waltrip found himself with a lap good enough to start the Brickyard 400 from the outside front row spot.

Left: Waltrip straps on his chrome helmet before the start of a race at Dover, Delaware, in June 2000. Below: Darrell stands alongside younger brother Michael at Bristol Motor Speedway in August 2000. The Waltrips are two of the most popular drivers ever to compete in Winston Cup racing.

teamed up with in 1981. As soon as he slid through the window opening of Johnson's Buicks, Waltrip was on to winning ways. The partnership produced three Winston Cup championships—in 1981, 1982, and 1985—and mounting the champion's center stage made Waltrip as loud as ever.

Waltrip left Johnson in 1987 to drive for Rick Hendrick. With Hendrick he scored six victories in 1989 alone, including his lone career triumph at the Daytona 500, the win he calls his biggest. By 1990, age and experience had toned Waltrip down a bit, so much so that he was voted Most Popular Driver in Winston Cup competition two years running. He was now the wise elder statesman.

Waltrip formed his own team in 1991, and right out of the box he established it as a winner. Victories came at Pocono Raceway and Bristol Motor Speedway as well as the Southern 500 at Darlington in 1992. Over the next few seasons, the team had brief stints of brilliance but just couldn't get it going. Waltrip sold his team and drove briefly for other owners, but with little success to speak of. On November 11, 2000, Darrell Waltrip ran his last NASCAR Winston Cup race, at Homestead Miami Speedway, and said goodbye to driving. Broadcasting is now his career of choice.

"Believe it or not, I have a lot of fun watching these guys race every week," Waltrip says. "Yes, I do miss competing against them. But I have seen times when I was glad I was in the broadcast booth and not on the track. Now, I'm enjoying what I do, but I wouldn't take anything for my career as a driver, because I was able to enjoy a lot of wins and three Winston Cup championships. Not everybody can say they did that, I guess."

Ultra
MOTORSPORTS
PHILIPS
SIMPSON
NASCAR
Winston Cup
Series

MICHAEL WALTRIP

15

Born:
April 30, 1963
Owensboro, Kentucky

Height: 6-5

Weight: 210 lbs

Sponsor	**NAPA**
Make	**Chevrolet**
Crew Chief	**Slugger Labbe**
Owner	**DEI**

Michael Waltrip is quick to tell you that stock cars aren't his only racing passion. The Owensboro, Kentucky, native has entered both the Boston Marathon and the Tampa Marathon. But it's in the NASCAR arena where his greatest talents lie, and like his teammate at Dale Earnhardt Inc., Kenny Wallace, Waltrip certainly knows how to hold court in any garage area.

The younger brother of three-time Winston Cup champion Darrell Waltrip, Michael is probably best known for his victory in the 2001 Daytona 500, in the 462nd start of a career dating back to 1985. The victory will forever be overshadowed by the death of Dale Earnhardt on the final lap—ironically, Waltrip was driving a Chevrolet owned by Earnhardt. He was in the lead, two positions ahead of the legend when the fatal crash occurred.

Waltrip returned to Daytona in July and finished second to DEI teammate Dale Earnhardt Jr. in the 400-mile event. Waltrip now has over 500 starts in a career that also includes 21 top fives, 85 top 10s, and 2 pole positions. Waltrip captured a second career victory in 2002, and once again the trophy was earned at the famous Daytona International Speedway. The win in the Pepsi 400 in July brought Waltrip some $172,000, and brought encouragement for continued success with DEI.

"When I first came South to follow in Darrell's footsteps as a NASCAR driver, I started at the top—even with my accommodations when I got here," Waltrip remembers. "I actually lived with 'The King' Richard Petty and his wife Lynda. A lot of great things have happened in my career since then, even though there aren't a lot of wins in the win column. But not everyone can say they've won the Daytona 500 but I can. So that's pretty special right there."

NASCAR Winston Cup Career Statistics

Year	Races	Wins	Top 5s	Top 10s	Poles	Total Points	Final Standing	Winnings
1985	5	0	0	0	0	395	49th	$9,540
1986	28	0	0	0	0	2,853	19th	$108,767
1987	29	0	0	1	0	2,840	20th	$205,370
1988	29	0	1	3	0	2,949	18th	$240,400
1989	29	0	0	5	0	3,067	18th	$249,233
1990	29	0	5	10	0	3,251	16th	$395,507
1991	29	0	4	12	2	3,254	15th	$440,812
1992	29	0	1	2	0	2,825	23rd	$410,545
1993	30	0	0	5	0	3,291	17th	$529,923
1994	31	0	2	10	0	3,512	12th	$706,426
1995	31	0	2	8	0	3,601	12th	$898,338
1996	31	0	1	11	0	3,535	14th	$1,182,811
1997	32	0	0	6	0	3,173	18th	$1,138,599
1998	32	0	0	5	0	3,340	17th	$1,508,680
1999	34	0	1	3	0	2,974	29th	$1,701,160
2000	34	0	1	1	0	2,792	27th	$1,689,421
2001	36	1	3	3	0	3,159	24th	$3,411,644
Totals	498	1	21	85	2	50,845		$14,827,176

Michael Waltrip pushes his Dale Earnhardt Inc. Chevrolet to top speed around Richmond International Speedway in Virginia in May 2002.

INDEX